MW00941860

1001 Nights

Twenty Years of Redondo Poets
at Coffee Cartel
1998 - 2017

Volume 1

Jim Doane and Larry Colker, Editors

1001 Nights: Twenty Years of Redondo Poets at Coffee Cartel
Volume 1, First Edition

Published by Redondo Poets, 2018

All poems used by permission.
Copyright to all poems is retained by the authors.

Cover design: Kit Courter
Front Cover Photo: Kit Courter
Back Cover Photo: Jim Doane

This volume is dedicated to Wanda VanHoy Smith, *in memoriam*.

Extra special thanks to Kit Courter.

ISBN-13 978-1985129641
ISBN-10 1985129647

Contents

vii

Foreword

Jim Doane

So every Tuesday night with the Redondo Poets has been a song and dance of the tongue, it's been a feast of words, it's been a poetic dinner show. it's been a spaghetti of sentences and a soufflé of emotions, a soft center of need underneath a crust of defiance. Always served in under four minutes.

To create a Tuesday night, we searched for the right ingredients. Tried this place, that place, finally the Coffee Cartel. Learned the art of choreographing the dance of readers, of showing up every week. Rain, traffic, marriage, cancer, unemployment, whatever; just keep showing up. One year, three years, take a break and Larry takes over, I come back, we join forces, ten years and we should do an anthology, fifteen years, twenty years and here it is. Crap, twenty years and we just kept showing up. How many times have I applauded to get here? Two poems, four minutes, 20 performers, intros, outros. Say 50 times a night for 50 weeks a year for twenty years. Fifty thousand rounds of applause. Other than the heart, poetry is hardest on the hands.

It has become all about the feels. So many new faces becoming features becoming old faces becoming memories becoming feelings. So to Jerry, Wanda, Craig, Barbara, Michelle, of course Larry, and to everyone who has ever contributed to a Tuesday night with the Redondo Poets, thank you for showing up.

Preface

Larry Colker

During the last twenty years, the weekly Redondo Poets reading at Coffee Cartel, in Riviera Village, Redondo Beach, CA, has featured hundreds of poets from far and wide, in addition to those from Southern California. This volume presents poetry by a few score of them. At least one more volume is envisioned.

We arbitrarily chose 1998 as the year the reading moved to Coffee Cartel. It might have been earlier, but the schedule of featured poets on the now defunct RedondoPoets.com website starts with October, 1998; so, there it is.

While featuring poets has been a fixture, the core of the reading is the open mic. Over the decades both the open mic readers and the audience have gone through many changes. But the primary character of the reading remains, above all, inclusive—of voice, perspective, age, subject matter, style, identity, and level of artistry. Eminent poets have featured at Coffee Cartel, but we are also always on the lookout for open mic readers who can carry a feature. Several such are included here.

Co-hosting the reading has brought riches to my life, and I am pleased to have the opportunity to share some of them with you in this collection. What I cannot share, though, are moments when a first-time reader reveals what she or he had never said aloud to others in public; when an established poet connects with an enthusiastic fresh audience; when a reader offers a prom invitation from the mic; when a performer carries us away with an original song; when a regular's work leaps into a stronger voice. You'll have to come to the reading for that.

Introduction

Jerry Hicks

Like a couple of male penguins sitting on a rock and hoping it will hatch into a baby penguin, Jim Doane and I set out to hatch a South Bay free-of-charge performance poetry workshop in 1996. At this time it was said: "The only audience for poets is other poets."

In the Fall of 1995, Jim Doane attended a novelist workshop I was hosting. He asked if I would comment on his writing. We talked afterward and I told him his poetry was somewhat short of stellar. At that point, neither of us knew anything about spoken word.

The next time I ran into Doane, he told me he was reading poetry in coffee shops. I was stunned because I was a frustrated fiction writer who had been struggling for 20 years to get recognition in all the conventional ways that existed at that time. I realize immediately Doane was onto something I had better do and asked him if I could tag along with him.

We first went to Sponda in Hermosa Beach. He read while I observed. On this particular night a woman had signed to be an open reader but when her turn came she was so nervous she couldn't read. The host asked the crowd if she could read with her back to us, and the woman was able to read all her poetry in that manner. It was a great lesson on how to be an accommodating host. Also, how gentle poetry crowds could be.

Jim and I discussed initially hosting a Saturday workshop for performance poets on the beach, but after going down to the beach and trying to read poems over the sound of the ocean waves, scrubbed the idea and settled for the first hospitable coffee shop we could find nearby: Insomniac South on Catalina Ave., in Redondo Beach. The place was so funky it had stuffed animal heads on the walls, but it was our place and we did our best to deal with it. The owner, Steve, gave us a lot of encouragement and advertising on his website.

We gathered workshop participants by talking to writers we knew and had met at various coffee shops; began meeting every Saturday starting at 10 am. And we had a microphone and sound system to practice basics reading skills.

We knew generally how to run a workshop as we started up, but we were finding only men to join, in spite of making a decision early on to recruit as many women as possible. Women who did come on Saturdays were so offended by our scene many would just rise in the middle of things and walk out. We were critical of each other's work in the same way poets were critical at the Thursday poetry workshop at Beyond Baroque and the Saturday workshop at Midnight Special. We were very up-front and honest. After each poet read, we gave both oral and written feedback. It became more and more valuable as time progressed and we collectively learned the nuts and bolts.

I knew Wanda Smith very well at the time, having been in the Millie Ames fiction workshop with her. Wanda had published three children's books but no poetry, and also protested vigorously she could not stand before an audience and read. Some other people in the Posse (as we called our group) knew her, too. All of us worked hard to entice her to come on Saturdays. She did, and became not only the key to the Posse's success, but also a linchpin. Soon after, Wanda brought in Eleanor Higgins and John Hutton. Jim Doane brought in Craig Anderson. Later I recruited Mary Palmer, a fantastic lyric writer. Jeni Bate joined us. The core group grew to twenty writers. During 1996, about 130 people at least sampled the workshop—most didn't adhere, as most didn't understand spoken word.

The first name of the workshop, coined by Jim, was: "The Posse." It was appropriate because in the beginning we spent a significant time attending as a group various poetry readings to learn what we could about Spoken Word. Jim found, and a lot of us read, *Aloud* from the Newyorican Cafe, a two-volume set of poetry from a year of poets who had read at that coffee shop. The set of books was nothing like the poetry we had been forced to read in high school and college, and one would doubt in 1995 any of it would be thought of as "literature."

Java Gardens in Huntington Beach was a major influence on the Posse. It was the first major venue where Wanda Smith and I read, both terrified that kids in the place would boo us off the stage because we were old farts. They didn't. They listened quietly, complimented us, and applauded like hell after we read—real authentication. Victor Infante and several friends, including Lob, set the tone (and the bar) at Java Gardens. It was a rowdy place with lots of young, creative kids and some very experienced young adults.

Charles Ellik hosted a reading in Long Beach, and the Posse went there often because we heard damn good poets who were not only entertaining, they were wise and very accomplished. Ellik had his own "posse" composed of local writers, many of whom also published poetry magazines. There were college teachers and students, playwrights, actors, musicians, street people, and ex-cons—all devoted to spoken word.

Ellik gave Jim Doane and me our first feature-poet opportunity, which we did, cowed by a woman who took the stage ahead of us and blew the crowd away. We couldn't come anywhere near her, but we got applause and the first item on the bucket list out of the way.

The Posse after two years of existence was little more than a microscopic spec on the vast iceberg of spoken word in Los Angeles. I estimated, based on distribution of G. Murray Thomas' *Next...* magazine, there were approximately 2000 writers active in spoken word. To support all that interest, there were about 15 major coffee shops plus bookstores, and active individuals supporting and helping poets get a start. Brown's Book Store in Laguna Beach gave each feature poet the opportunity to entertain a vast crowd of spoken word artists and a vast crowd of poetry lovers. Better yet, a nice poetry chapbook was also provided free of charge. For some poets it would be the first and last chapbook they ever had; for others, it would spur the poet to produce many, many more. Performing an initial feature reading and publishing a chapbook authenticated one as a real LA poet.

For five years the Posse, renamed Redondo Poets, met every Saturday, rain or shine, but times changed. We stopped growing in 1999. Larry Colker had joined us by that time; we had little idea how great his contribution would be later. Craig had gone north with his new wife Michelle (met in the workshop). People had returned to college to finish degrees. Poets had moved, or their drive to perform had been sated.

In 2000 a decision was made to keep the reading going and try to integrate the workshop with the reading. That notion didn't work as expected, but the reading continued to thrive. We had two fun reunions, one in 2001 and the other in 2002. John Hutton had created a RedondoPoets.com website. Larry Colker took that over and eventually, with Jim Doane, they became the driving force behind Coffee Cartel as a major LA weekly venue—shaping it as they went.

Wanda Smith never missed a Tuesday reading until 2016. She was 91 when she died in March, 2017, still writing poetry in the convalescent hospice up to her last hours. "I have to write, Jerry," she told me in January, "it's the only thing I do well." That was surely what any Redondo Poet could have said.

Afternote

This is a summary of what could be a book on all our activities. Hundreds of people donated time to speak at the workshop. Many, many people not mentioned here helped and influenced us. We did a great deal more than hinted at; traveled great distances to read to our peers, were active in poetry slams, and produced poetry shows. We met a lot of well-placed poets in our field and collectively published a great deal of poetry, including several hundred chapbooks. For most of us, being a member of Redondo Poets was life-altering.

1001 Nights

Twenty Years of Redondo Poets
at Coffee Cartel
1998 - 2017

Rachel Abril

Changeling

You looked different. I put my head on your shoulder
                              like things had changed.
        We stood in the grass watching the players
                        (we weren't supposed to be so close
                              but our shoes were entrenched
                              in the mud
                                    and the stadium
                                    was an opera house
                                    and no one quite knew
                                    their place.)
        So I held still because I was afraid you'd change back.
                              But
                              you got hit in the stomach
                              and so did I.
We should not have been so close.
                When I fly in my dreams,
                I hold my knees up so my toes don't touch the
                        ground
                And I clench my hands.
You changed voice.   It was strong
                              your hands on my arms on the park
                        bench
                It was dark and you talked different
                                          (I could hear you!)
                      I forgot it wasn't you and my face got hot
You looked different
        when you called me by our name
        and my pulse quickened because
                              my wide eyes could tell
                                          you had changed.

(I did not think I would be so afraid.)
In my most sincere moments you are there in my head
                    inside you is my laughter
                    when I didn't mean to put it there.
        You whispered in my ear
        That it was over with her
        And we ran through the dreamscape
        With Technicolor presence
        Until the morning lark
                    You looked different in the sunlight.

Unfound Unknown

The pilot's hair, slicked back like he's a World War II vet,
Unslick your hair, Lenny.
And oh, this has been brutal,
Come to 116 Otero, is Baby tryna tonight?
"Lenny over me? Well, damn," says the third,
Climbs through a window, oh don't do it,
Don't let the pilot have you, Baby.

Legs, propped up, chatting about cars,
Let's wrap ourselves in American flag streamers
And take pictures on the company camera,
But oh, shit, how the hell do we get this film out –

Letter from the driver, he's still sorry,
Can we call it bad timing and leave it there?

But Baby's kissing a World War II airman,
Back pressed into the bed frame,
The third storms out.

Go to the party, boss says.
She reads the letter, says it's beautiful,
Don't respond until tomorrow.

Or don't respond, ever,
Baby's nose is touching the pilot's,
Shivering as she hesitates, hesitates,
Does she know?
Back pressed into the bed frame,
Rough stubble, cautious grip,
And everyone, we're having a goddamn drink.

The driver's sorry, going to sleep now,
And the rum is gone, gone,
Mixed with the pilot's breath and
The cold chain on Baby's dog tag against his palm,
Holding the nape of her neck.

Still she can't decide, she doesn't know,
The third says not to leave,
But come to 116 Otero says the pilot,
And the driver, brushing his teeth,
Tired and off to bed, far from here.

Who is she kissing, the pilot or the driver?
Which of the two would it seem to be,
Or would that answer the question at all?
Baby can't quite place reality,
Or maybe it's just the syrupy chocolate wine,
Or the cheap beer, or the champagne –

And they're on Baby's balcony,
But she's tired, it's time for him to go,
Christmas lights in August speak the truth,
She'll see him in the winter.

He leaves, he winks,
It isn't over, and Baby's still unsure
Whether he's the pilot or the driver
Or both?

But the door shut an hour ago,
And Baby's just there by herself,
Unstringing Christmas lights
With a lingering note from the third
Slipped under her door,

Her mind on the driver,
Marks on her neck from the pilot.

And it really shouldn't,
But it all makes her smile.

E. Amato

Four Girls

I

No one ever taught Her how to be happy

She tries too hard gives up too easily
She's been bruised before
So why stick around to feel
that hard pit of disappointment
when she can just leave
Throw herself onto another acquaintance
like some kind of social disease

Moments like these she feels like cutting
Taking blade to flesh to stave off powerlessness

Wounds on her forearms heal and can be hidden
Wounds on her psyche cost her more dearly
Her writing descends further and further into sensuality
away from her heart's need for sincere intimacy;

But she taught me

Sometimes love does need to be tough
to stand up for itself in the face of aggression
Sometimes the universe puts up roadblocks
to teach us specific lessons
Which though invisible to her
are plain for me to see

II

No one showed Her how to be happy
facing the routine of a mother's beating
at the hands of an outraged father
Torn from nighttime bed into nightmare life
to be carted away—an orphan
One parent lifeless in a pool of blood
the other lifetime imprisoned

Imagine it
after that where could happiness fit in

So she writes and writes and writes these words
on pages cutting her story with ink into paper
Trying to dissect rage pain and shame
Without feeling them
Name them instead of dealing with them

but still the Words bring up the tears
of brutal years in a system designed to protect
yet constantly placing her in jeopardy
placement after placement
testing the limits of her frame
an obstacle course of abuse neglect and disdain
mocking the very definition of its name

Foster
          Care

If home is where the heart is
what do you call the place you sleep
stomach rumbling against a padlocked refrigerator

III

No one ever taught Her how to be happy
just how to go from welfare check to welfare check
letting love turned to hate
wrench your life into a wreck

She would do anything for attention
at 17 had already slept with more women and men
than I probably will ever
thinking sex was the mechanism to protect
against absent father
mother who just couldn't cope
but hope showed up anyway
in the form of brightly coloured thrift store clothes
and words she spits through ringed lips
to exorcise her personal bad trips

3 years later
she is just starting to look for normal
grateful for a little control over circumstance
healing her own wounds
by cleansing the ones of those who come after

IV

They probably told Her
she would never be happy
yet she is fighting herself alive
from an adolescence miserable and frightful
street urchin to collegiate scholar
she has etched her way into transcending the cycle

birth mother likely coerced into giving her up
for adoption to parents so irresponsible
she tended them and their natural children
somewhere underneath the question fuses
why adopt a baby you are only planning to abuse
but deeper deeper inside
she finds this incredible will to survive
to make herself a real life

she is my heroine
I want to show her to everyone
I tell her one day
she will be in the president's cabinet
with her mind heart and tenacity she can be in it
but more amazing
she will find a way to wake to the day
with a smile on her face

If it takes a village to raise these children
we are damn well short a few cities
But for every inch I raise them
They are even moreso raising me

So what I want to teach Her
Each her
Is how to be happy

Or at least that she can be

that it's our birthright to share joy and light
that every silver lining doesn't have to be hiding a mushroom
cloud
that living out loud doesn't have to mean screaming
that her life need not to be spent for survival scheming

that she has the right and the ability to thrive
that disappear us though they might like to

We are here.

It's a choice you make to love it fearless
All the courage that takes
is really what destines happiness as your hard-earned fate

Sketches of Pain

After 9/11
the only music I could listen to
was Sketches of Spain
Gil Evans and Miles Davis
creating sweet melancholy
saudade
over and over for two weeks
while I mourned
something I hadn't lost

Miles with his timbre and ambience
his use of the spaces between the sound
his intentional bending of tone to its edges
how I loved Miles

                        How I hated Miles
for back of his hand to beautiful cheekbone
his denigration of another artist female lover
his anger his insistence on being treated different
for being Miles for being male
for creating violence in equal measure to genius

Should I let James Brown make me feel good
forget the jail cell his wife sent him to
Let revolutionary poet move me who fathered a
movement though abandoned parenting
his own biological legacy
Gaze admiringly on a Picasso without asking
How many mistresses do you need?
                        And why do you paint them all so ugly?

What should we do
as woman
as artist
with this violent misogyny
this daily degradation
threat to intimacy and inspiration

we are meant to hold high idolize
turn eye blinded by brass knuckles and ring
turn other cheek blackened by inadequacy
Remain silent behind blooming lips

History will not be written by a bitch slap

Feminization will not be televised

It will be tweeted in ever decreasing blips
under radar quietly dots dashes and o's
silently it goes erasing victims and ho's
creating song of strong straight and bold

We are post-Oprah. We will not earn our stripes
from abuse and black eyes. Chris Brown's wrongs
will never equal rights.

                              We will fight.
The ways we know how
with know how and silent might
for every woman been forced
coerced battered or violated downright
facing that charming man—one hand
bearing artistry; the other sharpening knife

Men of talent with a knack
for the backhanded compliment
you are just draft dodgers faking yourself pacifist
then torching your asylums. We are tired
of putting out your fires.

You have ruined us for good men.
We no longer know how to trust them.
They have no patience for you either
so they leave us.

You are our unseen shadow
our lurker round every corner
we came to believe you were what we deserved.
You are not. You deserve only yourselves.

I can't forget Sojourner's truth just to get inspired
Can't watch trash talkers cash in on enlightenment
It is forever winter in our discontent
honour rent from nurturing breasts
Fierce the only medal left pinned to our chests
we are Precious we created you
we are not threatening your death

We are sketches of pain
secreting wounds in need of attention
turning confidence men in our own intervention
sequester midwive reinvention
resurrect from ashen corners
gloves off mouth guards firmly in place
wildly swinging
blows to the face
this time the soundtrack is Alice Coltrane.

You are our 9/11.   This is in our name.

Amy Ball

When I'm 764

One day, I'll have skin like an elephant
and forget to wear underwear
routinely
  (oh well)

One day, I'll remember some of the things I wish I could forget
Like the disgusting taste of black licorice jelly beans
  (Mom's favorite)
Or vomiting chocolate donettes and salsa after too much beer
  (freshman mistake)
Or the specific weight of Mama Kitty's head in my hand, after the
vet injected her with morphine. I held that weight of that gorgeous
cancer-filled body until her tiny paws and lungs and heart entered
an infinite pause
  (I kept holding)

Still, one day, (I know) I'll feel solidly eight foot three
  (even if I've shrunk to four foot eleven)

One day, my reflexes may be inadequate on a softball field
but will be enough to keep me from breaking my ass on the stairs
  (if I'm careful)

Maybe I won't mind
that those kids just look right through me, and think I don't know
  (anything)
But something about the way that boy has his lanky his arms slung
around her tiny shoulders in front of the junior high will make me
remember Brian Lloyd's handwritten note
  (check *yes, no,* or *maybe*)

16

And I might remember Brian Lloyd, or forget Jesse Carmichael
        (or vice versa)
I never liked either one of them as much as I liked to eat mochi
Which will probably sound good in the days when I still have all
of my teeth
        (mostly)

Somebody might look at a picture one day and say
Man, you were pretty
And I'll think, *I still am* and
Maybe you don't even know what that word means

But that'll be okay
I'm sure I'll forget it, as soon as it's said,
since I'll be noticing just how much fun it is to be in this moment.
And then this one
And then this one
        (even if fewer and fewer people notice me there)

No matter
A few lucky people will see how brightly I glow when they look at
me out of the corner of their eyes
Maybe one or two will notice that I don't even use my feet so
much anymore
        (due to the fact that I'll prefer floating by this point)

When I'm four hundred seventy-two, who's gonna need feet?

People might observe a little bit of a stoop in my step after so
many years,
        (*Poor thing, Life's been so hard*)
But they'll be getting it wrong

If I'm slightly stooped and forgetful, it's probably because

I've been spending all of my wisdom growing these
blessed wings

And they're a little heavy
        (but glorious)

I wasn't focused on longer eyelashes
or better breasts
        (though it was briefly considered)

Yes, I've been working on these feathered things
these gossamer steel, flexible fire, whimsical dreaming pulsing
wings
(just under my skin)
This skin—wrinklier still, in order to hide the magic of this life
Just under the surface
        (I've been storing it there)

All the love and the joy and the leavings, all the pushing and
breaking and breathing
that could have collapsed an average girl.
I've been pulling the long shadows of life and the great bright light
into these hidden
iridescent
wings
        (You just wait)

When I'm three foot seven, I'll be ninety percent wing.
And when my soul no longer has need of this body,
When I'm six hundred thirty eight
        (Or so)
I'll leave what's left of me
and I'll fly away.

I may not remember a lot of things specifically
        (hopefully, I'll remember you)
But, no matter
Every lasting moment
        (however fleeing)
will have a single feather
And every single feather will beat
thousands of singular, various beats
on a cadence with the rise and fall of these wings
Until my whole life is just a rhythm
of lifting, pulling! A whoosh of air on your face
my soul throwing its arms into the sky and giggling
lifting, careening
listing, floating
bursting forth into the blissful everythingness
that is all around us, at all times.
And me,
carried by the wings of this one and glorious life.

Oh, Amy, you say
That's such a long way off now

Oh, Amy, you say
Tomorrow, you should focus on your taxes

Oh Amy, you say
You're still young now

And I say, *Yes*
Yes, I'm still young now

But I will
And I do
Remember this

Your Bicycle's Name Is Natalie

I said we couldn't leave until we saw a fish
We rode our bikes down to the beach, recklessly

past your apartment, we once shared
past our old grocery store, and coffee haunts

I'd already had too much white wine
But it was Sunday and you are beautiful

I stood in the water and didn't mind
that it came up and soaked my shorts

Distant wildfires behind us
The setting sun ahead

Everything in between was smoke
and observation. Even us

You took videos of planes overhead
My eyes never left the waves

Three dolphins and a sea lion later
My feet were covered in sand to the ankles

Until a single swimming flash
in the middle of a backlit wave

"Did you see that?"
"Did you see that?"

It was miraculous, to have seen
together, a fish in wave

I imagine that fish laughing, crashing towards the shore, and swimming for her life.

Ellen Bass

Reincarnation

Who would believe in reincarnation
if she thought she would return as
an oyster? Eagles and wolves
are popular. Even domesticated cats
have their appeal. It's not terribly distressing
to imagine being Missy, nibbling
kibble and lounging on the windowsill.
But I doubt the toothsome oyster has ever
been the totem of any shaman
fanning the Motherpeace Tarot
or smudging with sage.
Yet perhaps we could do worse
than aspire to be a plump bivalve. Humbly,
the oyster persists in filtering
seawater and fashioning the daily
irritations into lustre.
Dash a dot of Tabasco, pair it
with a dry martini, not only
will this tender button inspire
an erotic fire in tuxedoed men
and women whose shoulders gleam
in candlelight, this hermit praying
in its rocky cave, this anchorite of iron,
calcium, and protein, is practically
a molluskan saint. Revered and sacrificed,
body and salty liquor of the soul,
the oyster is devoured, surrendering
all—again and again—for love.

The Orange-and-White High-Heeled Shoes

Today I'm thinking about those shoes—white
with a tangerine stripe across the toe and forceful orange heels—

that fit both my mother and me. We used to shop like that—
trying them on side by side. That was when there still

was a man who would cradle your heel in his palm
and guide your foot. Sometimes he would think he made a sale,

only to have one of us turn to the other—
and he would have to kneel again, hoping to ease another naked
    sole

into the bed of suède or leather. I thought those shoes
were just the peak of chic. And—my God—

you bought me a pair of orange cotton gloves to complete the
    ensemble.
Why is there such keen pleasure in remembering?

You are dead ten years. And these showy slippers—
we wore them more than half a century ago. The first boy

had not yet misted my breasts with his breath
and you were strong as a muscled goddess, gliding nylons

over your calves, lifting your amplitude into a breastplate.
Who will remember these pumpkin-colored pumps

when I die, too? Who will remember how we slid into them
like girls diving into a cedar-tinged lake, like bees

entering the trumpet of a flower, like birds disappearing
into the green, green leaves of summer?

Michelle Bitting

Lupercalia

The ides of February are brutal.
Love's sticky sentiments
gumming up the air
make it harder
to breathe. Gilded truffles
snug in their cellophane tombs
dare you to pluck them
from underworlds
and eat. Hearts dangle
in pharmacy windows
pretending to pump real red.
Brutal for a boy who feels
but won't say
what it is to be sixteen
and never one secret admirer,
never a glitter doily
or silver Hallmark
waxed with lipstick's
smoky kisses. What ghost
can this mother conjure?
What diaphanous caress?
When in Rome
and if long ago, I could run
naked through alley ways,
my breasts swinging
like fevered trolls,
like devil bells bared,
tolling resident evil. I could
don a goat-skin cap,
carry my pot

of flames to the desert,
burn salted meal-cakes
with vestal virgins
and raise them
to the stars,
to dead crows
and broken Caesars. But
it wouldn't change the fact
of his incomplete beauty,
how girls turn away
when he opens his mouth to speak
a sound less than smart.
Won't change the fact
of his gawky bust
and uncommon sense,
an art far too wild
and no longer cradled
in the cave of a darkened living room,
where once we rocked
and he suckled, at times, stopped
to let glide
the nipple from his mouth
and look up at me,
just look at me...
his future,
his mother
and unconditional lover,
his only Valentine.

Joni Mitchell Is Not Unconscious!

She hasn't fallen into the coma
those nasty tabloids suggest
She's alert and well and sitting up
in her bed at Cedars Sinai
I was walking on The Promenade
in the land of palm trees and Saint Monica
where sun and blue shade duke it out
wending a path between bass clef and treble
and then I saw it: JONI MITCHELL IN A COMA!
And I said No! Not her! Maybe it's true
she's been a recluse for half the century
in her pink Bel-Air mansion
Our Lady of the Spanish Canyon
where she chain smokes and is paranoid of everybody
especially the invisible parasites
like colorful irritable fibers
she's convinced bloody her skin
make her tear all her clothes off
and slither like wind on ceramic tiles
Who wouldn't believe aliens
were camping in your private parts
when there's Paparazzi spying
from the Hydrangea everywhere you go?
There is no rain in California
and I have been to Hollywood parties
and done perfectly disgraceful things
But Joni Mitchell is not unconscious!
She is still here in the in-between
going up and down like her melodies
make us when the heart is shadows and light
and we are desperate to be forgiven
Oh Joni keep singing we need that nothing gray about you

Laurel Ann Bogen

I Dream the Light of Reason II

The Reasonable Woman is a hope chest, a locked cabinet.

The Reasonable Woman is pleasant enough.

The Reasonable Woman is the converse of sex.

The Reasonable Woman is a durable good, a sound diagnosis.

The Reasonable Woman is a subordinate clause.

The Reasonable Woman is childproof, although Heidi is already
    up to her knee.

The Reasonable Woman is a skillet, a war bond.

The Reasonable Woman is a fugue heard on the intercom.

The Reasonable Woman is a graph of stock options, the
    percentage of return.

The Reasonable Woman is open to suggestion.

The Reasonable Woman is a string bean, a cauliflower, a field of
    potatoes.

The Reasonable Woman is a packet of Alka-Seltzer in the
    Accounts Payable file.

The Reasonable Woman is considering bankruptcy.

The Reasonable Woman is a stacked heel, a running shoe.

The Reasonable Woman is a pair of pantyhose in the bathroom sink.

The Reasonable Woman is fat free.

The Reasonable Woman is a shadow of herself.

Why would The Reasonable Woman become unreasonable?

May 12, 1971

Mornings starch white
the rumple of pastel sheets
two figures angle
and stave off encroachment
the sun blinks above canisters
bodies snap to attention

they move without collision
smooth and defined
collars and buttons contain static

it is 7:34
a Wednesday

the figures compact themselves in chairs
there is coffee and stock reports
it is cheery like this
the day propped before them
like the Wall Street Journal

the solidity and logic
of the counter is interrupted
only by a wedding band
in the soap dish
and a pair of scissors
to cut coupons out of skin

she says she has to do something
he says that would be nice
and his vacant sky falls to linoleum
the short breath of morning
bustles questions into kitchen corners

it pats the figures on their hands
and says "there, there dear, it's all right."

Lynne Bronstein

The Day of The Surgery

Dawn came late
At almost six thirty,
Dark clouds with sun piercing through
And fog obscuring the street signs.
We got lost while driving
To the hospital,
Olive View.

I was still me, smiling for a photo,
Sitting on the
Examining table.
Then I had to say goodbye
To the loyal friend who'd brought me
And left my inhibitions
Behind with my clothes,
Obediently donned
The backless gown
The too-large slippers,
Plastic cap over my hair,
And electrode stickers
All over my body,
Buttons that pushed at
My nerves.
I thought myself ugly and grotesque,
Not to be looked at.
But this wasn't prom night.
Those things
Were not to be thought of now.

Lying on my side I glimpsed
On the monitor in hazy blue
My heart via what they called
A cardio echo.
It was not shaped like
A valentine
But was almost square
And I saw flashes
Of what looked like lightning
Amidst the thunder clouds
Of cardial tissue.

I did not see
The damage of lost love affairs
Or career rejections.
It was a lonely organ,
All business,
Knowing only its own life,
While impacting mine
With its unexpected speed-ups.
I could see no
Traffic jams there
The streets within the heart
As foggy as the streets outside,
And likewise, no guide
To location,
No signage I could read
To find out what was wrong.

Hence the surgery
For which they now laid me out on a table.
A needle in my arm,
And all wired up and connected.
A sedative rushed into me.

All was dark for a moment.
A minute, a quick space in time
That I did not exist.
I did not even dream.
I thought how relaxing and wondered
Out loud when they would begin.
And the doctor said
It's already over.

Two hours had passed.
No abnormal pathways
In my heart,
Electricity normal.
Everyone so kind and nice.
I thanked them all.
I said
When I get home
I think I will play the song
My heart will go on.
And they all laughed.

In the meantime
That square and lonely organ
Remained that way,
Did not turn into
Anything red and frilly,
Trimmed with lace.
I was alive, I had been spared.
I could look forward
To life.
And if my heart indeed
Would go on
Would there be hope
For electricity there

34

Of a different kind,
For lightning bolts
And floods of sun
Through the morning fog
And all that makes
The hearts of the young
Beat faster without the risk.

For is this all
That the older are saved for,
To read the instructions,
Take the pills,
And tread carefully,
Taking the lightning in little doses
To sustain for another year?
Two years or forty more
What difference if
No shocks
Occur and days
Are quiet and safe
Without sexy heroes
And embraces to make us blush.
The Bride of Frankenstein
Comes down from her pedestal,
Flaunting her electrodes.
She wants to dance all night at a disco
And wants her lover to hold her tight
Even as they both go up in explosive smoke.
I said I want some dessert.
I want erotic spark-inducing chocolate.
If earthquakes and car crashes
And heart attacks can happen any time,
Oh dear God,
Why can't love?

Unsent Letter

You are contrary.
Do you know that?
No.
You don't.
You sent me an email of about thirty words
To tell me you were too busy to see me,
Or talk to me,
Or, apparently,
To congratulate me
For my new book.
Everyone else I knew
Wrote: Congratulations!
One word
That takes up less room
And less time
Than the words and time you took
To tell me you were too busy.

You said you were inadequate
To fulfill my needs.
You made it feel
As if I were not fulfilling yours.

You said it was not me
But you.
So you admit
You have failings.
But you want to stay a failure
Rather than try to improve.

Let us go back further.
You said

You were afraid.
But you wanted to go forward
And see what would happen.

You were still being honest then.
And I found it endearing.

Most recently you said
It would just be too crazy,
Too busy,
And you would not have the time
To talk much to me.
Not much.
Which is not the same
As not at all.
You could have said a great deal
In "not much" time.
You could have said
Congratulations.
You could have said
I love you.
You could have said
Marry me.
You could have said
Be with me for the rest of my life.

I could have said
I love you
And I could have said
Go to hell you selfish putz.

I have nothing
More to say at all.

The next quote
Is up to you.

Elena Karina Byrne

White Doll

> *The real history of consciousness starts with one's first lie.*
> —Joseph Brodsky

I lied to the mirror
holding my only Barbie doll by the pink neck,
her fixed eyes open, parents
in the other room.

There was a commotion
of high radioactive-white clouds thirsting above and my body
way down below with the dusk hour's inconsolable
light between the furniture.

Somewhere, behind the fish tank
in the first knuckle-blue darkness where doll slept
on the bare floor, you could see my brother kneeling

in the clockwise picture, in the weathervane away place,
see the drowning world there always in mourning,
        hurtling itself free from us like endangered bees
from a broken jar. At that point

everyone remained silent in the house, listening to
day and to night. I could do anything
        and it wouldn't matter, all child, feeling

both boy and girl full of fear stories no one told me
to tell, the doll body, shiny
        and insufferable as the future.

On Deaf Ears

> —*believing as I do that man in the distant future will be a far more perfect creature than he is now, it is an intolerable thought that he and all other sentient beings are doomed to complete annihilation after such long-continued slow progress.* —Charles Darwin

North of the Chimney Swift's swerve, sperm champagne or
the Herring Gull's rail against another costume dusk, beach-goers
   who pee
in a beer bottle borrow Beethoven and cannot engage in
   conversation.
      We'll find the death headlines stuffed pointblank
        between mattresses
and the smock coat laid out for the next art project backtalk.
   A woman in another
country has no say. Here, you are offered moonlit food on
   sandstone's cockcrow
or black lacquered plates, the image of the mouth left on the
   mug's wide rim
of blue glass. Next year the water temperature will rise and rise,
      fish will be responsibly fished in Darwin's darkroom and
        guess
what, Twilight of the Gods and cold laws of physics will come.
Doctors will tell you something soon you don't want to know.
The Dead Zone's baleful bale of dry hay. Typewriter F key
   broken
and swallowed with a lump of licorice. Such taste contagion
will kill you, along with sugar's slow toxin lifting the spirit
demographic. But still, still, there is poetic license and a fork
      someone provided to make music.

Michael Cantin

This is THAT Love Poem

You know the one I am talking about.
This is THAT love poem.
This is the one where the speaker attempts
to transcend cliché
and touch the truly sublime.

Oh, how he will struggle to ignore the pull
of a watching moon.

Oh, how he will lament that he cannot
address her aquiline eyes.

No-he must avoid the obvious.
So instead he will watch her sleep.
Note the constellations of freckles
that adorn her too pale shoulders.
He realizes that he craves to tangle
his fingers in the matted birds nest
that is her bed head.

He spends the entire night pining,
failing to find the proper inspiration
that will prove his poet's worth.
He stares intently until sunrise
paints the rise of her ass—
how like a perfect peach,
round, with the most tiny
translucent hairs…

He is breathless as the morning dawn
ascends perfectly between those twin rises.
He has grown ravenous,
as he descends,
mouth open,
to take a bite.

Bohemia Comes to Redondo

Toto is whisking us away to Africa;
the music smooth and lingering,
a perfect accompaniment to this
tall glass of Clontarf on the rocks.

I am surrounded by the shapes of poets,
strange disambiguation of concept,
the profundity of the mundane,
this wooden table.

I am being coerced to write
as I pour freehand unto the yellowed page
some Guinness,
Spam?
I warm my speechless throat with liquid fire.

You can't smoke your cigarettes inside.
It isn't allowed.
The tea drinkers are now the new rebels.
When did it come to this?

How de Sade must surely weep at this scene.
He no doubt misses Justine.
Here in the amber gloom we search in vain
for a reason to cry,
or a reason to dream:
for a reason to sleep no more.

All well drinks are $5.00 after five.
Self respect costs extra.

Hélène Cardona

Woodwork

If I could gather all the sadness of the world,
all the sadness inside me
into a gourd,
I'd shake it once in a while
and let it sing,
let it remind me of who I used to be,
bless it for what it taught me
and stare at it lovingly
for not seeping out of its container.

Life in Suspension

Let me introduce myself.
I'm the Memory Collector, your companion and spirit guide.
Let's unwind the clock, peel the past.
The reflections you give me, conjure, surrender from within,
I throw into the fire, the cauldron of resolutions.
They burn into embers and flickers that evolve into butterflies.
They flutter away, free and heal of all strongholds
so they can revisit and reinvent who you are.
Let the dance begin.

I'm in my mother's womb in Paris.
She's scared. I want to get out.
I'm three years old in Terracina, Italy, sharing a room with four
    girls.
My grandfather visits from Greece.
He holds my brother on his lap
and says, a boy at last, I'm not impressed with girls.

I'm four years old, in Monte Carlo.
My mother takes me to school.
A pigeon poops on my scarf.
She reassures, it brings good luck.
I'm five years old, in Karben, Germany.
It's Saint Nicholas day, my birthday.
Marieluise feeds me Lebkuchen, Stollen and Pfeffernüssen.
They taste like heaven.

I'm six years old in ballet class in Geneva, breaking my point
    shoes.
The Russian master ingrains in me the correlation
between pleasure and pain.
I now know the two centers sit next to each other in the brain.

I'm seven years old, in the Swiss Alps, making
snowmen, skiing, hunting for Easter eggs.
My mother laughs then says, your father can't be left alone.
I'm eight years old, in the Jura mountain, in love
with my dog, playing chess with my dad.
I'm ecstatic.

I'm nine years old.
My grandmother takes me to the market in Tarragona
to buy the bitter and pungent quince she craves.
I'm ten years old.
My cousin drowns me in the beautiful blue waters
of the Spanish Mediterranean because I threw sand at him.
My head hits the hard bottom, all the air's gone from my lungs.
My last thought is, no one knows I'm here.

I'm eleven years old.
My mother makes jam with apricots, strawberries, peaches and
    plums.
She's filled the house with the intoxicating scent of gardenias.
My brother throws another temper tantrum.
I'm twelve years old in math class, mad with laughter.

I'm thirteen years old.
The Music Conservatory in Geneva is sheer magic,
an enchanted world I inhabit alone, the key to my soul.
My piano teacher has such faith in me.
I'm fourteen years old, between worlds.
My aunt married a fascist. He grabs my dad by the throat.
It's the middle of the night. It's loud. I can't sleep.

I'm fifteen years old, in Northern Wales,
riding a fabulous horse along stunning steep cliffs,

racing him to full gallop in bewitching Celtic wind,
relinquishing cravings in the dust.

I'm sixteen years old, off to San Diego.
My mother cries at the Paris airport.
She breaks my heart but the pull is stronger.

I'm learning to let go, trust the ripeness of the moment.
That everything happens at the right time.
To appreciate what I have.
I'm connected to my bones,
filled with the richness and texture of space, uplifted,
vibrating, reverberating. I become the sound
of Tibetan bells, echoing and hovering in the cosmos.
I perceive the whole world below, life in suspension.

Randy Cauthen

from *Slow Night*

One dawn outside Patna
a spider had woven
astride the wheel.
Thin spokes of the web
between those thicker.
It was gone, that spider.
The cart moved, the web turned
flecked with dawnwater.
Having been spun
by what was gone, it turned;
droplets moved inward
and outward moving West.
I was called away for a time;
day rose; it was gone.

from *Slow Night*

Sandstorm west of Anxi.
We hunker down five days,
mouths pressed against
the overfull wineskin
of the earth. Elsewhere she
writes rewrites a letter
that will go unread, or
looks down a little looks
to the side infinitesimally
(her hands moving) embarrassed
to be pleased at something
someone has just said. Wind outside
throwing the particulated world
around like a thousand thousand little
deaths. All of her beautiful small
actions taking place somewhere
unknown now, taking place everywhere.

Sharyl Collin

Velveeta

When I was in the 3rd grade,
I had to write a paragraph
about my dinner the night before.

I wrote about Spam,
and the way my mother
had drizzled Velveeta over it,
when in fact, we'd been out
of Velveeta for months.

I never told anyone
I'd made it up,
having fallen in love
with that Velveeta-filled world,
wrapped in a hug so rich
it could warm any truth
set down on the shoulders
of an eight year old,

a place I still imagine
a golden embrace for all that I am,
when in reality, without Velveeta,
I'm more like Spam,

held together by compression—
a peculiar collection
of muscles and tendons,
pounded into shape
and made palatable with salt
and an over-exuberant laugh.

I Want to Know

I want to know the meaning
in the tilt of your chin,
to anticipate the humor
in the gleam of your eye,
to give weight to your sincerity
when your brow is raised.

I want to know the place
your stories are stored,
walk the aisles and run my fingers
along the bindings,
learn which was embraced
and which was read just once
and then set down for good.

I want to know the language
of your scent, let it tell me
when you are hungry
and when you are full,
to know the weight of your arm
on the slope of my back,
the sound of your voice
when my head rests
against your chest,

know your rhythm
and balance, roll and thunder,
feel the coil of your tension,
watch your anticipation
when it moves in me.
I want to know
the sound and shudder
when it all lets go.

Brendan Constantine

A Giant in the Field

I don't think I ever caught his name, I was a child
and he was just another grown-up, a minor god
of some grey pantheon. I don't know why I was there
but I guess the babysitter was busy. I wore a clip-on
necktie, and I can see my 'good' shoes flashing under
a table. It must've been a company dinner, something
for my father's work. An emcee spoke from a podium,
made jokes I didn't get, but I laughed anyway because
my parents did. Their laughter was a thing I liked
to ride: a wave, a wagon. There was big food and
cigarettes, I remember staring at some anthuriums
and thinking how ferocious they looked, how like
dinosaur flowers that might spit poison if you
got too close. And that's when the guest of honor
was introduced as "A real giant in the field" and
I looked up, over all the dark heads, ready to see
the giant, ready to see someone truly enormous
wearing a boat for a hat, or eating a whole cow
like an eggroll, making great big footprints
down the aisle. But it was only the man I'd seen
before. Maybe the giant was still in the field. Yes,
that was it; this man was here to accept the award
because the giant was busy, standing in wheat,
or maybe cotton, which I'd just learned about
in school. He had to stay in his field, waiting for
bad children to walk by, so he could offer them gold
or beans or a chance to save their lives. But couldn't
this guy handle it instead? Surely giants can have
a night off to get a trophy. The kids in the field
would still get what they deserved. Alas, no giant

came to the microphone, just this wimpy God
saying Thank You and sweating. I remember
he cried at the end, how he used one finger to stop
a tear, a gesture I later copied. I did it this morning.
The news was on, there were pictures of smoke,
a woman turning rubble with her hands. I'm not
sure what occurred but there were sirens and
a whole house flattened by something huge,
something that had moved on.

Kit Courter

The Dark behind the Dude

Michael is the sort of crazy, mixed-up dude
that is astonished by his own shadow.

Not because of the shadow, but because
of the eyeball, the eye that can see
the shadow. And the mind
that can form and understand
the image, the heart that can feel
and feed the mind, the lips
that pass food, the tongue that tastes,
the throat that passes and closes, the stomach,
guts, anus, the whole damn chain, including
the bones and muscles, skin that make up Michael
so he can look down on the sidewalk
and see that, indeed,

he got in the way of the sun. That is
the sort of crazy guy Michael is. I mean,
last week, he set off in search
of sub-atomic particles. Not because

of the quark, the gluon, the neutron,
or even the atom, but because
of Avogadro's Number, the huge
counting of atoms that make-up
DNA, the way RNA copies to make
proteins, the way proteins make women,
he went because so many women
are beautiful, he went for art,
for smooth curving lines and bold tones,

for a book of Edward Weston's nudes
he picked up at a bookstore in town. I mean

Michael, the man, understands
scale, he sees people, but he also sees
society, he sees humanity, he sees
a planet bustling with action, attraction,
division, concision, uniqueness,
how he stands out in the crowd, but not
because of Michael, but because of the crowd,
because if it weren't for the crowd we wouldn't have
an economy, we wouldn't have population,

we wouldn't have little towns spread across the prairie,
we wouldn't have the lunch counter in
a little Nebraska town where he and I met one day
to suck straws dipped in chocolate malts,
because of the malt, because of the wheat,
because of the Kansas dry-land farm, the tractor,
the fuel, the ancient Paleozoic life that became
trapped in rocks, petroleum, the light that fell on leaves
that rotted to become the oil, the sun that sent the light,
the atoms that merged to emit the light,
the whole damn chain!
of how, because a trilobite sneezed,
somehow Michael was formed from a sperm and an egg.

California Laurel
(Umbellularia californica)

Clapboard cabins
            in Santa Anita Canyon!
sash windows,
panel doors,
tar paper roofs — hard to see
            at a distance —
      covered with drifts of
lancet-shaped leaves,
      shrouded by dense
         lancet-leaf trees! — Leaves dark green
      with spots of gold —
California Laurel —
   "Balm of Heaven"
— Sierra Madre's medicine chest.

Put some leaves against your temple
to ease your aching head;
smear the oils on your skin
to keep infection at bay;
gargle the tea
to relieve sore throat;
decoct — and wash your hair
to be rid of lice.

It's a magic tree,
a healing tree   when taken
      in moderation
— though you must take it with care —
                  for too much of it
can return you to your gods.

Melanie Dalby

Нормально (normal'no)

for Russia

in America, when you are asked, "how are you?"
the average response is, "good."
in Russia, the average response is, "Нормально."

It's been two weeks in Russia. An unexpected winter's chill,
reminding me that summer was home and I was not.
I come home from school. In the bathroom, our hot water is still
off so my hands are cold against the soap.
My host mom is sitting at the table. My skin prickles from the
moment she says, "О, Мелани…" and from there fast Russian
slips from her lips just like the tears down her face and I'm trying
so hard to understand what she's saying but it's like trying to catch
fireflies in a jar without a lid
I catch a word for it to fly by and I comprehend that someone has
died but I don't understand who, but I feel her last sentence, **Не
знаю когда моё сердце перестанет болеть**, that she doesn't
know when her heart will stop hurting.

how are you?
in America, we answer that we're fine, we're good,
even if it's just a tiny bit of a lie.
a little lie, no more questions.

It's been two hours since my host mother told me, alone in her
apartment, that there had been a death in her family.
There's a gathering.
I shut myself in my room to do homework, to leave them be.
I still don't know who it is.

But I'm not going to ask for clarification, not now, the proper way they told us to ask if we were confused, **Простите, не всё понятно- ещё раз, пожалуйста, помедленнее, кто умер?** Excuse me, I didn't fully understand- one more time, a little slower, please- who died?
No.
First to arrive are the granddaughter, Liza, and daughter, Anya, who picked me up from our first excursion and who helped me buy Internet access and who took me shopping when I told her I wanted to find a **маленькое чёрное платье**, a little black dress.
Liza joins me in my room. I let her, even though now she's been told not to come in without asking. I figure she doesn't understand and is scared. She's only six.
We sit quietly and work on our respective projects- me, grammar, and her, coloring. More people arrive.
My host mom's parents, her sister and husband.
I hear the clink of china teacups, the nice ones from the cabinet in her bedroom.
Soft murmuring.
And, just once,
Just once,
sharp powerful sobs of the truly grief-stricken.
It's maybe five seconds.
It sounds young.
I think it's Anya.
Liza leaves the room to check, comes back,
says nothing.
I don't ask.

how are you?
Russians say they are "**Нормально**"- they are normal. This is the halfway point between good- **хорошо**- and bad -**плохо**. our definitions for the same word are a little different.

It's been two weeks since The Death. I still have no idea who exactly it is, but I know it is a young man whose portrait we keep in the main room with a candle, an icon, and a piece of **чёрный хлеб** on top of a glass of vodka.

I know he died too young.

I know he is related closely to Anya and my host mom, but Liza never cries and Anya never cries where people can see and my host mom hasn't cried since that first week.

Anya and I are alone in the apartment for a week.

We are talking one night about anything and everything- family pets. Liza has a cat, six month old **Хася**, who was a gift for **Новый год**, New Year's.

Anya tells me Liza wanted a cat and kept asking and asking for one, and finally for New Year's her dad gave her a cat. I ask, joking, if he didn't like dogs. She says, No, no, he really liked dogs. Then she pauses.

You know, she begins, that someone died a while ago?

Yes, I say.

You know it was my husband, Roman?

The clock ticks. Our tea steams. Anya prefers Earl Grey, but I hate it. I am stunned.

I- yes, now I do, I say.

Yes, she says, fingers light on her tea. She is calm. He was just thirty years old. He had a heart attack.

The atmosphere is quiet and a little painful in the way that sadness hurts like an old bruise behind your heart.

I tell her, if you want to talk about something else, we can.

She says okay.

how are you?

the American base line is good.

the Russian base line is normal.

this is something you need to understand.

It's been three weeks since the Death.

I'm watching Stanley Cup highlights and Liza watches over my shoulder.

First she asks if we are watching футбол- soccer. I say no, hockey.

"Папа любит футбол и хоккей," she says.

Папа любит, любит, he loves football and hockey
he loves, loves
not любил, loved, he loved football and hockey
he loved, lived, past tense
she didn't say любил, loved
and not for the first time I wonder if she knows.

how are you?
in Russia, "good"- хорошо- is not a lie.
if you say you are good, then you mean that you are feeling good.
something good has happened.

It's been six weeks since I arrived in Russia, four since the Death, and only two more weeks until we leave.

Danila—our Russian friend, who speaks about as much English as we speak Russian—spreads his arms wide, the sun glinting on his hair and borrowed Raybans, the sliver of a breeze that comes by every so often making the heat against the packed dirt road bearable.

"This is Russia," he says, spinning on his heel. The quiet, endless fields, the forests in the distance, the daisies on the side of the road.

He says, "In English you have- мало- мало слов-"

"Only a few words," we supply.

"You have few words. Beautiful, pretty, perfect- и всё. But in Russian, we say прекрасно красиво блядь как охуйтельно эта природа блядь." His version included several Russian swears.

Looking at the spread of land and sky he's gesturing to, I want to retort and say he's wrong, we have the words in English, we've got more words for beauty than just three- but I can't think of any just then.

We walk on.

The wheat and the sky stretch on as far as the eye can see in every direction, giving the impression that we're looking through a fish-eye lens falling toward the earth, that we're swimming through God's great big sunny blue bowl. No sound but the soft roar of wind through grass, not even the chittering of insects. Just the perfect sensation of being alone. Just four Americans, one hungover Russian, and the clouds. We're still walking.

how are you? как дела?
i'm breathing. normal. **Нормально.**

Dust to Dust

they say we're made of old stars.
they say all the elements of the universe repeat themselves in you
and in me.
the iron fillings in my blood that were once shards of supernovas
are drawn to you like you're polarized
pulling a haze of life up underneath the blanket of my skin
i commit to a blush that i cannot hide
        an assault the hue of baby's breath and roses
           of sunsets and sunrises
                of a spot at the edge of the world i've never
                been to but the carbon in
                    my bones remembers.
i shake with the fire of nebulas.
please look at me
        please look at me
            please look at me
i'm hiding galaxies beneath my breastbone and stars beneath my
tongue
lightyears separate your bones and mine
even when we're too close to breathe apart.
the air in our lungs forms auroras in the frost.
i tap constellations
        old new and invented
           into the void of your back
i swirl nebulas into being
        from the stardust i trail
           like ink in my fingertips
i am painting the milky way from long forgotten memories on
your skin in luminous strokes, a map to call our forgotten
elements back from their long journeys across solar systems.
i dip my hands into the clouds where stars are formed and cup
promises in my hand that shine with light already a million years

old. i tip my palms over your head. star light with the weight of
angel feathers. trailing down your neck, the sifted silver sounds
like the tail of a comet heard in the delicate curve of a shell. it is
enough to smother our whispers in velvet. the ruffles in your hair
are like canyons, running wild with comet dust that makes you
cold to the touch.
i am filling you up with beauty.

      beauty you forgot you had, have, will have

          across all the eons your particles have traveled.
millennia from now, the earth will remember the swirl our bodies
make, a supernova burning its way through to my core that wind
will trace like scars in the sagebrush.
(in my quietest moments i miss you like a black hole.)
the hooks i carved for you in my palms will remember your
gravity in indelible ink we bled from the crescent moon when it
had no more to give.
our bodies were once the same star. my atoms will find yours
again, if you want it.

      if you want it.
(i am drawn to you like a moth to an abyss,

      facing down inevitability from a boat made of all the first
      stars we ever wished upon.)
we are a compass pointing further North than dreams can find.
Cassiopeia, Orion, Ursa Major and Canis Minor find their way
home through us

      a Polaris rooted to the strength of the earth.
the constellations are drawn to your eyes.
i gather them close like daisies from a meadow, like all the words
i save for you tucked inside my cheek, like bodies gather stardust.
i only end up pulling you closer.

Amber Douglas

Minty

just like her the ceiling is topless / the walls are climbing doily's
    ripped lace
painting nude the color of obnoxious / just like me / your guts are
    twisted & twirling caught by knowing
I'm next door / welcoming her when ego engages your vicarious
    wit / just like a wish
she has a magic white collar wick pressed with denim leather
    silicone busts melting away the burn
as our lips meet while we both swallow the worm / just like words
    that flew by flippantly
she wants & is another place / time for tea
just like mover & shaker coffee shop doors open / malignant
    maneuvers alter your mind filter broken
just like me / you require expressive bold dark grinds / just like her
she is where even floors shine back an agreeable crowd
an espresso double cuff digital wink- wink selfie - flashing loud /
    just like you / she won't discourage abuse
just like me / power is an after effect aroma / teasing & tantalizing
just like her / not relating / the real is moving too fast for retreat /
    just like her
attraction greets laughter you won't forget / just like me
her head's packed with gummy bear syrup eyes / calculating
    moral inventory
always on alert for surreptitious surprise / like coming of age lust
she anticipates listening to well crafted highs / nearing comfort's
    edge / an anxious fear
that you & me & she will show up here
just like we all play different movies in our head
just like this time Donnie Darko isn't dead

Spaceship

I gotta try to come back down
she says you gotta come down sometime

but why, do you really have to come back, so soon
after shedding, molting losing side saddles and leaving anchors

eyes hypnotized by the stillness of vibration
.... oh
      here we go
captain oh my captain
we. have. lift - off!
so weightless & indescribably liquid
buzzing an absolution for addiction
this freedom from gravity

eight seconds tilted right
contemplates to calculate perceptions
temporal, dental, pre-frontal and primordial lobes
this narcoleptic neurosis wants to study it's chemical alchemy
just to feed curiosity when the triangle chimes

eleven eleven the algorithm blinks on the left side by side
gone .... gone .... gone
spinning merrily going round the absence of thought
sliding down a tube of infinite sheet glass

was it enough, is it ever enough, are those the constraints
is that the complaint, having access to just enough
leaving that craving always needing
so it may continue to grow into its knowing
why i must come back down

the transition traps the distance
this is a love bird lined by the wires
telegraphing a high for the mind
mid addiction, in the infinite
is it ... are we... brushing fingers meant to make it linger

I gotta try
she says
you gotta come back down sometime

John FitzGerald

So I've been working on these *Title-At-The-Bottom* pieces
and up to now have only two.
You know at every reading there's this moment
when the poet steps up to the mic
and begins to break the ice with jokes,
or thanks those who made it possible,
or other readers, or all of you for coming out,
and sometimes, like now, if you're lucky,
the so-called poem will have started
before you noticed and is over. Painless. Okay.

Enough Fooling Around

By the way,
that's the title at the bottom:
"enough fooling around"
is written in here,
and so is what I'm saying to you now.

The Next Poem Is

The Man Who Knew Everything

Sapiens number seven billion.
And it's the same with me as with every other human.
I formed immersed in a dark sac of fluid
and bore through a tunnel into the light.

From that time I have never been alone.
From that time too I have always been.
I am a hypothetical being.
Every person born of my line

the day and year and place that I was,
and given my features, strengths, and limitations,
would almost certainly be me.
For over a year did I write certain nights when I could.

Orator for the planet with a voice like dirt
and a few odd ghosts behind me.
Herein lies the testament of earth,
a statement much too much for me to bear.

It overwhelms me, and I am afraid.
I have no proof.
I am poet and cannot explain.
I will go into the other room to drink.

My God, my love is way out of control.
All manner of loneliness I pray to.
I will be like the far thoughts of paper.
When the word existed before it was spoken.

Amélie Frank

Bonobo Face

Yesterday, a Dinah Shore smile
sunny crinkles at eyeliner's edge
mild loosening of the jawline
the comfortable shrugging
and acquiescence as Girlfriend
Time spots you an espresso.

Today, the squint in sunlight
has given way to pools
of lividity and infection.
The nose's coordinates
are now smothered in edema,
road rash, and a
Todd Browning retribution.
The smile is a beestung stoma.

She will live.
She will never blink again.

Pitiless is the veil separating
the quotidien yesterdays
from the unasked-for present
lousy with Internet trolls,
tentative plans for
the reconstructive altar,
and the persistence
of Lucy Grealy's ghost.
And yet, she is optimistic.
Perhaps she does not
realize enough.

Perhaps knowing everything
is beside the point.

For the last five weeks of her life,
my sister knew little but agony,
intubated, aching, and
deprived to the end
of comforting flavors,
reassuring textures,
the singular satisfaction
of swallowing,
and the companionship
of her own voice.

Yet, I suspect even she
would have declined
the offer of a lengthier life
beneath that veil
and she would have continued
down her own appointed
and abbreviated path.
Better the devil who has
dogged your steps for 17 years
than the devil who makes that
once-in-a lifetime drop-in,
tosses you a poisoned kismet,
and cleaves your lengthier days
clean down the middle.

Such unmindful randomness.
Or, worse still, such savage karma!
If fate makes you the bride
of the rough beast
what the hell, then,

with truth and beauty?
Where does the
peaceable world reside?

Girlfriend Time passes you
another espresso and says:
"No one asked Frankl, Reeves,
Sadat, or Mandela for permission
before their lots were drawn."

Emblems of Conduct

for Adele Slaughter

Here is the deal, Alma. We won't speak the names out loud. We will whisper them to each other when the time comes. Your job is to keep me from becoming sidetracked by my humor. My job is to speak the truth to you, to assure you that what you suffered from was neurasthenia, a nonsense disease ascribed to bright girls from whom the wrong things were expected and to whom the right things were denied. Nobody suffered as much at the hands of small-town doctors as the bright girls did, Alma. You were far more observant than you were ever given credit for, and like every small-town Cassandra, you were ball-and-chained to a nonsense disease. No wonder the girl you were had to burn away entirely that harsh summer in order for you to survive. Me, I burned for nearly thirty summers, twenty-five before I even realized that I was on fire. I know that seems like a lot of time to you, but your lifespan is a two-act play. I have been around for fifty-six years. It took a long time for the good, sweet girl in me to evaporate.

Alright, Alma. Now you whisper the name of your crucible boy to me, and I will whisper the name of my crucible boy to you.

(Listen.)
(Whisper.)

Give me your hand, Alma. You loved him more than any cool drink of water, any slice of frosted cake, any burst of your favorite color, any perfect day, any song hummed to you by your mother before she lost her marbles, any handkerchief redolent of your favorite sachet, any moment that your father told you he was proud of you, any archangel, any notion of perfection and the hereafter *precisely* because that boy was who he was. He was a sharp boy, a hungry boy, and you understood him. He was an imperfect thing, an arrow whose trajectory was well off the mark, but you loved him for who he was, and in the most secret cache of your heart, that was plenty enough for you, for the girl you were before summer burned away the anima of Alma. On the surface, you seemed to have become carnal, selfish, perhaps even cynical. People are so quick to ascribe bitterness to maturity. They mistake the slow pace of recovery for lassitude and indolence. But the truth of the matter is that you saved your most secret self, and you began to feed her. And that was an absolute good. We cannot feed love to others if we are not first fed ourselves.

So tell me, Alma. What is the name of your new love? And I will tell you mine.

(Listen.)
(Whisper.)

I crossed a contested borderline in order to be with mine, Alma. There are those who would judge me for the choice I made, including myself before my many summers of immolation. But the days of Thermidor have tempered both of us, and I suddenly found the muscle to step over the line when love was offered to me for the first time in twenty-one years. I know, I know. That's a lot of two-act plays. And I know, that's my humor cropping up again. Forgive me. I had to be fifty-six years old before a man looked at me and told me I was beautiful. I had to be fifty-six years old before a man said, "I have fallen in love with you, Amélie." And he said it first. And I was so tired of being The Brokenhearted Girl that you, more than anyone, can understand why I had to step over to the side where he stood. As with you, summer had to end for me some time. It is a day-to-day thing with my new love. And it is not in any way ideal. But someone holds my hand, just as I am now holding yours, and someone thinks

74

about me and misses me, just as that handsome stranger outside the casino is surely thinking about you. You understand love better than most, Alma. Don't let any academic knothead tell you otherwise. Oh, you see? I made you laugh. Good for me. Good for you. Conduct yourself with a heart full of love, Girlfriend. Display no colors, no adornments but your own. There is no sin in knowing better. There is no sin in survival.

(*Emblems of Conduct* was the original title of Tennessee Williams' play *Summer and Smoke.*)

John Gardiner

In a Nutshell

How strange to realize that my mother
was hydrogen, my father was helium,
and all the other elements of my being
came from a super nova, including
the pine tree outside my window
with a hawk hovering above,
and the cone that just fell will have
the same effect as the super nova
in its finite purpose to seed and create,
and that is the sum of all things
in a nutshell, which also serves a purpose
no greater or lesser than my own.

Kiss the Whore

It would be no surprise if women sensed him coming,
the whore-man who slept with dozens of whores
in their houses of ill repute: Moonlight Ranch,
Mustang, 7th Floor "Fun Room" at the Mapes Hotel
where he found a kind of whorish love reciprocated
and because she wouldn't charge him,
she lost her job. She fell in love with innocence,
big mistake for a whore to make,
all this before his 18th birthday, a rite of passage
in the city of trembling leaves.

Whores never kissed him on the lips. They would do
everything else in his imagination or theirs,
but they never kissed him. Professional courtesy.

They're the assembly line in a factory, and endless workers
punch in and punch out on their time cards.
You might call them moveable feasts.

Should the opportunity arise,
he will kiss a whore with all his heart and soul,
forgive her everything, even what she won't forgive herself
and hope she'll do as much for him.

In the Match.com world of today,
we pay billions of dollars to test the waters
for love and sex, sex and love,
for love we can only imagine,

but what we really want
is for love to imagine us.

Jessica Goodheart

My Doorman is a Poet in Need of Praise

He wears silk shirts under his blue doorman's jacket.
His knee never ceases to jiggle under the table of his night.

He lights imaginary cigarettes with the fire in his eyes.
Doors are like books that he opens

books that he closes. When we come in laughing
on Saturday nights he looks up at us

through the winters of the last century,
his mind a full boat of immigrants.

With packets of coffee shop sugar, he builds temples
to an only-sometimes god. To the blue-bearded panhandler,

he offers coins from his childhood.
To the fourth-floor poodle salt biscuits of silence.

Mornings, he stands so that we may wrap him,
tree-like, in the colored lights of our praise.

All he asks is that we commit to memory
the luster of his brass buttons, the creased landscape

of his forehead, his tangled eyebrows,
his fingernails of amber.

He is not practical like the super, not rich like the owner,
does not squander words like the postman.

But when he greets us, the whole city
tips sideways and water drains from the alleyways.

Refrigerator Day

in the full bright air conditioned hum
of my refrigerator day
are moments of triumphant scouring
call it progress

moments too when I want to
throw down my sponge and doze
curled up on kitchen tiles
letting mold grow green and wild

Branford Goodis

Flowers, Staples, Crackheads, and Cream Cheese

I was a flower delivery boy
one summer
at Joe DeVivo's shop.
His face was permanently numb
from cocaine.
No matter the hour
he slurred his words.
Little mustache and wavy lips
tripping over themselves
as he mumbled and cursed and screamed
rambling nonsense
that was both hilarious and terrifying.

Joe DeVivo was insane
and I admired him for it.
Donny was his partner.
A fat old Italian man
who looked like a retired mobster.
The two of them sat there all day
clipping the stems
and creating colorful arrangements.

Patty lived above the shop.
She inherited millions in the 1980s
when her parents died,
but spent it all on drugs.
Now she was broke,
wandering around in her nightgown
with no bra or underwear on.
When she came in the store

Joe DeVivo would lift her gown up
and try to put staples
in her ass.
Her pimply tits flopping aimlessly,
and her hairy bush
shamelessly curling out toward her hips.
Joe DeVivo loved that stapler.
He would storm out
of the bathroom
sniffing and twitching,
coke snot dripping down,
and swing that stapler
at anyone in his way.
He would grab me by the wrist
looking for my veins.
"Wat da fuck's da matta,"
click-click-click
Three staples in his own arm.
"See ya little pussy…
it doesn't even hurt."

Every once in a while
he'd send me off to deliver a bouquet.
I was only seventeen
so each drive was an adventure.
I would glide through
the suburbs of Philadelphia.
Rich, polite, smiling people
receiving sweet-smelling gifts.
And then I'd return
to the coked up
stapling madman.

One day Joe DeVivo
tapped Patty's phone line
so every time she got a call
it rang in the shop.
We'd put the call on speaker
and listen and laugh.
Patty had a boyfriend named Q,
a toothless crackhead with a lisp
who stumbled in and out of the store
and smoked cigarettes on the corner
while eating stale pizza.
Patty had another guy on the side,
a repulsive degenerate
who called himself Cream Cheese.
He was an amateur porn star
known for his twelve-inch penis.
He told me a disgusting story
about how he once
fucked a woman in front of her husband
in Los Angeles,
and came so thick
with such power
that when they found out
he was from Philadelphia they said,
"No wonder…
you're squirting Philadelphia Cream Cheese."
And an amateur porn star
was born.

And so it was at the flower shop.
Ridiculous characters coming and going.
The stapler snapping
his hungry jaws.
Loud snorting in the bathroom.

Fat Donny with his mafia glasses
snipping and snipping
the stems.
And then these peaceful drives
through twisting hills
of mansions.
Flower arrangements
buckled in every seatbelt,
sometimes leaning over
and spilling water
on my seats.

One day I came to work
and there were a dozen cop cars
surrounding the building.
German Shepherds on leashes.
Boxes being cut open and inspected.
It turned out
crazy Joe DeVivo
was dealing coke in bulk.
There were pounds of it
in the basement.
And he was laundering money
through the store.

When I got home
my mother was gone.
I had the house all to myself.
I opened my drawer,
pulled out the stapler,
and clicked one
into my arm.
I stared at it for a while
in disbelief,

then dug my nail under
and pulled it out.
Two little red dots
seeped blood

like a baby snake
had bit me.

Joe Devio was right.
I was a pussy.
It didn't hurt
at all.

Kiss me Katrina

Hurricane Katrina
passed over Miami
before making its way
to New Orleans.
She was only a Category One.
Slowly,
delicately,
calculating her destination.
Sharp and sexy.
Dangerous.

The University of Miami
was locked down on Thursday
so everyone bought bottles and cases
and by the time
the storm hit at midnight
we were drunk
and brave enough to come outside.

Everyone was in their bathing suites
goading the storm.
Daring it to dump
tropical fury upon us.
Two dozen students in the quad
of the on-campus apartments.
One of the girls rolled out Slip and Slide
and we all went head first.
Hair whipping in the wind.
Lightning snapping palm trees.
Thunder rumbling the ground.
Tremors running up through the blood stream
and tickling the heart.

Ten of us split off
and went for a walk.
Bathing suits and beer.
The sky spinning.
Palm trees stuck in sustainable gusts.
We came upon
the outdoor professional pool.
A tree had fallen on the fence.
There was an opening.
We climbed over,
lifting the girls,
landing in knee deep water.
The pool was overflowing.
The waves were bobbing,
slamming into the clubhouse.

And there it was,
rising up,
ten meters above,
illuminated by lightning,
blurry through a million blades of water.
The high dive.
We all instinctually began to climb
like ants going up a picnic basket.
Shanking and shivering,
slipping and catching ourselves.
The wind getting stronger
with each step.

I watched the girl before me
jump
and get blown sideways.
Oh, how terrifying and beautiful it was
at the top of that high dive.

Looking over the flooded campus.
Thunder and lighting and swirling clouds.
Palm trees holding on
by the fingertips of their roots.
And Hurricane Katrina
with her little opening.
Her beautiful black eye.
You could see into the depths
of her soul.
A window to the universe.
A few stars sparkling through.

I ran and leapt.
Falling with the raindrops.
Frozen in air with gravity.
Frozen in the moment.
Then silence underwater.
Twelve feet down
my feet touched the floor.
Nothing but the sound of bubbles
until I emerged,
inhaled to the chaos of everyone screaming
and celebrating.
We didn't die.
We captured her.
Held her for a moment.
Our lips came together.

We were one.

Over the weekend
Katrina took it slow over the gulf.
Gaining speed and crashing into
New Orleans.

Breaking levies and homes.
Raping and murdering.
The city underwater
begging helicopters for help.
And if you go there now
it seems as if the concrete and wood
will never dry.

But I remember Katrina
when she was a young
and mischievous girl.
Before she became
what you know her as today.
And I'll never forget the freedom
I felt,
and the way her breath tasted,
and how wet and wonderful
that moment was.
Frozen.
Falling.
Nestled in the eye
of her storm.

Tresha Faye Haefner

The Jungle Tattoo

The man who lived in this apartment before me
painted the walls dark green so they would look
like the deep round "O" of a forest pool in shade,

but really, they remind me of the man himself,
who, upon handing me the keys, had said
he had lived there ten years, alone,

that the neighbors were quiet,
but few of them friendly,
and I should keep to myself,

then had turned down the hall, revealing,
through the cotton white lucidity of his shirt,
a back covered by the tattoo of a tiger

whose black eyes stared out
from a tapestry of jungle vines,
emerald embroidered branches,

snakes like strings of topaz undulating
away as if lunging after the man
down the white florescent-lit hall.

And I want to ask him now, as I sit on the couch,
rubbing my thumb over the needy brown upholstery
watching lights go out

in the darkness I have inherited,
if there is something that made him need to cover

nakedness, like loneliness, in color.
 At what point in his ten years alone
did he decide on that tattoo?
Was it in a moment like this

when night's charcoal shadow was closing,
like a hand, over the yellow light of lately lit apartment windows,
and the walls were going black,

in spite of the color, that he went
to have his body soldered by a solid reminder
that something could exist in absence?

That the dark unholiness of a body,
with its isolated, heavy-metal sting of solitude,
purple bruises, and blood dark songs, could also be

the dark web of trees, a river, red flowers, green leaves spread
so wide they might shelter things, like dew drops and pollen,
the rock-round back of beetles, waking in the dark to flap

their wings through the heartless black, unafraid, so that when he
    would fall
back into himself, alone, in this room, he would land,
like that tiger, two paws dug into the solid earth, able

to look up through the lucid green embroidery
of the jungle's never-sleeping leaves, to find
even the inside of himself, still illuminated by stars.

I Will Arise Now and Go to Los Angeles

After William Butler Yeats

I will arise now and go to Los Angeles
where the lip gloss is leopard print
and the eyes of women shine like jewels waiting
to be excavated from an urban jungle.

I will arise now and go to Los Angeles
where they sit on hundred dollar bills,
and dream about coconut water
and hours of easy money in their sleep.

I will arise now and go to Los Angeles
where everyone spends Saturdays
on the cliffs of the Palisades,
the windows open and the sun smiling,
on two dollar bottles of coke.

I will arise now and go to Los Angeles
where the surf on Venice beach
prays for dolphins, and Raga music, and incense burning
in the breeze.

I will arise now and go to Los Angeles,
where four a.m. wake up calls and want ads and asphalt
pull everyone from their beds like music.
Where even the barefoot men
soak up rays of the sun, and spend their days
juggling rainbow colored hacky sacks for cash.

I will arise now and go to Los Angeles,
Who is a stranger with red hair, who says she's an actress
with rose petals crushed into her pocket,

or the boy who pays rent by playing songs
on his sad red American guitar.

I will arise now and go to Los Angeles
Where anyone can stop on their way home to stand outside of
    Mann's Chinese Theater,
and put their feet where the stars have stood,
and watch the Magnolia blossoms open and fall like spotlights
someone is casting down for them alone.

Dina Hardy

Yours Is Everything

Hers is dedication to dead brother
Hers is exact weight and material
Yours is word as hammer you swing
into parallax light
Hers cliché to say cliché but cliché
His personal pronoun verb article noun
verb temporal clause
His is cut the first six
then another six
Yours is everything is cut petals
by quinary-colored insomnia knife
Hers and his are student
His and hers are popculture reference
Theirs are slang & song lyrics
Hers is woman is moon
His is rhetorical millisecond
His is not bad
Hers is lunch order lottery tickets
Yours is five syllable pixel afternoon
gathering sunflushed desires into
swandive ink bouquet
His is letter to someone famous
Hers a brand name
Look at them
Who they know
What they see
Yours is architecture in erasure
entire city apparition quicksilver life
Welcome

[the magician's assistant]

Heavy, flowing garments kept women from being magicians' assistants until the end of the second war. Emancipation for all. Here, wear these trousers. Climb into this box.

I climb into the box. Simplicity cubed—until the sound of the saw. Love is such an illusion. The moment when the body is divided by desire. Half in love, half not. Which half, crazy? Ophelia wrapped the weight of fear for a love not returned around her shoulders, slipped (ambiguous) into the water, an aqueous solution. Slid under. Her billowing shroud, & gowns & gowns & gowns in the currents. Wet black pixel hair.

Rue in the ruse that turned ruin (definite). I walk into the waves. What parching madness, what weight this stone, in stones. Love—heavier than any object when, with sleight of unseen hand, replaces anxious secrets in hidden pockets.

Donna Hilbert

Madeleine

I think of you lying on the couch,
days after the birth of our boy—
your grandson—how your sobs
awakened me from fitful sleep
that first morning home.
You'd come to care for me, the baby,
your bewildered son.
Between the tears you said that no one loved you,
and now, surrounded by all this life,
you felt still more alone.
I watched you cry
as if watching a foreign movie,
in a language I couldn't speak.
I searched for meaning in what I saw:
your hair the color of bourbon
in the almost empty bottle
beside you on the floor.
I watched your face, still beautiful
un-mottled, smooth.
But I listened un-moved,
while you complained that I failed
to appreciate all you'd done—
marigolds planted by the back door,
the freshly laundered sheets.
Later, fueled by still more bourbon,
you started a fire
drying socks on the old gas stove.
I told your son to send you home
or I would take the baby and go.
Deep in my fertile life

I couldn't fathom such unhappiness,
didn't know the other meaning of passion,
had no language for such hunger,
had no language for such grief.

Domestic Arts

I am a young mother
so bored staying home
I agree to play Bridge
with my neighbors,
whom I suspect put up with me
to find a fourth to fill the table.

They are goddesses of domestic arts,
and between games hold forth
on finer points of decoupage, macramé
and the transformation of cans
into casseroles.

Still I am smug,
for I have gifts of my own:
precognitive dreams
and gift of the phone,
which I demonstrate by chanting
Mother Mother Mother Dear
call me now while my friends are here,
and when the phone rings
they are believers.

Because I love an audience,
I tell them my dreams:
how I see trash cans burning
the night before they burst in flame
behind my house,
how Papa's heart attack
awakens me from sleep.
How I knew the night before she labored
Jan's baby boy would be born dead.

98

Now the neighbors play three-handed games—
Pinochle, Euchre—
keep their children indoors,
cross against the light
when they see me coming.

Jean Barrett Holloway

When the Shadows Run South and North

Spring 1956, Kwajalein Island

There will come a morning
you will waken in darkness—
your mother will shake you before it is light.
There will be no breakfast,
but you will dress for the day
and walk without speaking down to the lagoon.

The stars watch you walking,
your mother, your father,
the Southern Cross hides below the horizon
from the camera your brother
has brought to record
the untimely flight of the shadows of night.

Blackness, then bright light,
then bigger, the sun in the north.
In silence the shadows run back and forth
from the noon in the sky.
In silence your faces
are lit up with fusion, camera snapping its witness.

In seconds the shadows flood back.
You walk home without talking,
no sound but the crunch of your shoes on the coral.
Electric lights watch you
as you eat your breakfast
then stop as the thunder at last shakes your ground.

The immediate fish
and the birds are fried,
intermediate sea life is cooked on one side.
The camera records
the sand on the beach
looking the same as before they died.

There will come a morning
you will waken in darkness—
and the sun will arise before it's supposed to.
There will be no breakfast,
no pictures for scrapbooks.
In silence the shadows will run back and forth,
in silence the shadows will run south and then north.

After Reading Nadezdha

How did it all begin, the silence and the frenzied lying?
—Nadezhda Mandelstam

We arrive
tourists in a dream without color,
our minds
outside all that occurs
but it happens to us anyway.

Step into the hotel lobby
with baggage,
expect (snap of the fingers) help.
Reception does await
but there is a line.

Some of those ahead are dressed
a little differently.
Pajama bottoms here and there, beltless pants.
Here and there a woman with her legs
against the wall, bosom straining against --

The queue moves. Glass disappears.
Hallways proliferate. Rooms without windows but
too many doors.
Sense of arrangements, aware
of being observed. Their eyes move, not their heads.

Our display: try to seem good.
Widened eyes, helpless hands in laps.
Watch the one near us, the one behind the desk
inside the room with the excessive number

of doors that open—

The one playing the part of the human being
leans in so sincerely, asks as the others
—our companions have been taken away—
watch. Their display: license, a hairy hand
sharking around the doorknobs.

Submit. Pass the quiz,
confess the names or make them up, pass
to a higher level of deportation… incarceration…
Oh to turn back, to wake again before
these insufficient answers and the question.

Eric Howard

The Fates on Location

> *Something bad is going to come of this.*
> —Richard Nixon

They were tired of crowding into taxis that smelled of
    cigarettes and so many transitory lives reminding them that
    they were legally blind and could not drive in Los Angeles,
    tired of wearing the same clothes at 2 A.M. that they'd put on
    day before,

tired of filling out expense reports for the shadows surrounding
    those photographs of the senator on the concrete floor,
    grimacing with his legs splayed,

of being kept awake by crickets even in third-floor hotel rooms
    in the middle of the city,

of ensuring that William Barry tell him, "No, it's been changed,
    we're going this way,"

of hanging heavy crosses on the shoulders of seventeen-year-old
    busboys who happened to be shaking Bobby's hand the
    moment before,

of tending to all the details like steering the crazy shooter who'd
    gotten drunk toward the hotel coffee urn rather than the back
    seat of his car to sleep it off,

of rosaries pressed into dying hands, of suit coats put into use as
    pillows, of guiding bullets with awful grace into five bystanders
    exactly as required,

104

of hearing Bobby ask "Is everybody OK?" his blood slowly pooling
on the passageway floor between the steam table and the ice
machine,

of the war ending him rather than him ending the war,

of cameras that can't run backward, and the reporter asking "Is it
possible?" into his reel-to-reel tape recorder,

of the silence of the young campaigner in her straw hat holding
her face in her hands,

of how weak they felt knowing all the rolls to develop, frames to
count, and final cuts to be made,

how they'd have to fly across the country to guide his funeral
procession through a shantytown called Resurrection City,

how they were getting older all the time while the job kept getting
harder, and they had to get in the taxi and keep going, day
following day with death their unobtainable goal

LeAnne Hunt

Good Intentions and Cracked Pavement: The Importance of Smiling

I set out to be clean.
If there is one thing I know,
do-overs exist only in make-believe.
Scars are impervious to erasers,
and water cannot remove shame.
No one has ever seen me
unbroken.

My mother wanted me to be happy.
Everyone knows
I am faking. My smile slips
between cracks. My mouth
is the fault line in the terrain
of family.
You will never see me fall
again.
My bones grind under crumbling
infrastructure.
You thought me spineless.

We were the worst possible outcome
in a double blind, one-sided study.
I'm certain of nothingness,
of the gap between intention
and perception, of the wasteland
between should
and could.
If I were in charge, the moon
would spin out of orbit.

I cannot hold anyone together.
If you were here in this house, I
would be underground.

I set out to be good.
I set out to be pure.
I set out to be happy.
I set out to whole.

Naked Dreaming

I dreamed of being naked,
        but no one noticed.
I spent the entire dream
        hurdling over obstacles
                to find my pants
but tripping on each task—
        each request   more ridiculous,
        each interruption   more absurd.
Wait,   there's an exam, and I don't have my pants
        or a pencil?
They are all going to notice   and laugh at me,
but they never do,
                nor do they see my panic.

"This is a dream about being unprepared,"
        you say.
        "Are you stressed at work?"
I can only nod.

Another friend tells me   it's about aging.
That past thirty, we are
                invisible to men.
Where once we cringed at catcalls,
        now we grimace at "ma'am."

My mother tells me   I am hiding again.
I used to stash candy
        until summer and the spreading neon stains
                spilled the jellybeans.
I drew floor plans   with secret staircases
        and trapdoors.

My fairytale castle   had a moat
          and a maze.
I never wanted to be found.

I can be emperor   if
       everyone closes their eyes,
          and if
      I close mine hard enough,
I can be the air.

Elizabeth Iannaci

The Eldest of the Twelve Princesses Tells...

After seeing what he'd seen,
clad in his shadowy nothingness,
following the twelve of us, night
after happy night, you'd think,
after watching us—faces
hot and wet as bath stones, hearts
pounding the Mazurka's 170 beats
a minute, hair rivuleting down our backs;
after hearing the concert
of our laughter reeling high and wide
off the ballroom's vaulted ceiling;
after holding our shoes—
our paper-thin soles in his hand—
or, after he'd won and chosen me,
                        at our feast,
                                our wedding ball,
me: bouncing in my seat,
tapping my fat-soled slippers;
him: taking my knife, and then my fork
from my hand as I conducted
the Contradanse;

after knowing all that,
you'd think he'd at least take me
dancing. Nothing fancy:
a Valse à Deux Temps,
                Varsouvienne,
                                Quadrille?
But no.
I suppose now, he'll be a decent king—

having tiptoed to the throne
he'll never tip his hand; finding music
in the marching, the hoof beats of war,
he's practiced at ducking into shadowed
alcoves to avoid the embrasures.

And us? Perhaps even before I came
across the dark weft of the cloak,
hidden in the lid of his crusty old trunk,
before I marveled at how I could
not see my hand as I held the cloak,
perhaps, even then,
I had already become invisible to him.

All In the Timing

*The symptoms of Retinitis Pigmentosa (usually
noticed in children, adolescents and young adults,
with progression of the disease continuing
throughout life) include loss of peripheral vision
and night-blindness.*

When I was a child I was seen
not heard, like the moon
or a good servant. I was told to
watch my mouth; wondered
what it might do. I took to
carrying a little mirror.
I listened to my heart—heard
da-dum, da-dum, da-dum, da-dum—
it taught me perfect meter, began
my life-long fascination
with drummers. I tried to speak
when I was spoken to, and only
in short, controlled bursts:
        Yes, Mrs. No, Sir.

When I was a child I was all ears,
dogs spoke to me in a language
I knew. My grandmother's Collie,
Prince, who slept in a barrel
turned on its side, told me *Go Away.*
I ignored him. I still have the scar.

As a girl I was blind to meanness
and let anyone pull my leg. Later,
I wore my heart on my sleeve.

It was right at everyone's elbow-
level. So tiresome, always
cleaning up the mess. In time
I began to cover it with sweaters.
Coats.
As a young woman, I discovered
falling in love is all in the timing:
Colin was married when I was blind-
sided by his electric green eyes—
20,000 volts. My IQ would drop
40 points whenever we were
in the same room. The same
city. I'd become a fool: put on
my sweater backwards, miss
the flight, lock my keys in the car.
Years later, seeing him, hearing
that voice, again, electromagnetic
shock. This time I had a husband,
Colin was newly single. All in the timing

like selling a stock or telling a joke—
Two guys walk into a bar.
You'd think one of them
would have seen it.
For years love would descend
upon me, wrap itself around me
like darkness, swallow me
whole. Once, it took me over
a decade to fight my way out
of its paper bag.

Now, as my vision closes in,
darkens at its edges, the world
around me becomes less

inviting, seems to have more
sharp edges, potholes,
sudden obstacles. Now, I listen
for unexpected skateboards,
joggers, baby strollers. Now,
when men ask me out to dinner,
a movie, offer to help me take off
my coat, I mostly decline. Mostly.
I'm chillier than I used to be,
and it really is all in the timing.

A blind girl walks into a bar...

Charlotte Innes

I Sit Still and Something Happens

In the late afternoon light of the exhausted room
with its years of scratched floor, leaking walls
inadequately patched, crumbling in summer heat,
a mote of happiness floats in like a suicide attack.

Where did you come from, sudden annihilator?

Did you sneak in on my black cat's paws?
On the back of a fly lazily surfing the breeze?
Did you look at me green-eyed? Or wear orange,
like that girl swaying in a dream down the street?

Maybe you've always been here, lying in wait

for a certain conjugation of light and breeze
lightly touching my arms and legs,
stroking my neck, kissing my face, whispering,
*love is like that, an unpredictable
invader,* insisting, *I'm here, let me in.*

My Friend the Philosopher

My friend the philosopher sees his brain as a map
some nights, with all the grief in the world
laid out inside, little pink and blue
countries, like candy wrappers, waxed papers
laced with poison meant to kill a child.
His head aches with weighty continents of pain

for history's pragmatists inflicting pain
regretfully, in the interests of... On maps,
in books, he tracks with markers like a child
every erasure of faith or race—worlds
away from the present, until the morning papers
hit the mat. A bombing in Iraq that blew

up kids for being there. Or boys in blue
shot by boys in red, immune to pain
almost, who almost want to die, for the papers—
to be mourned, my friend says, to be on the map
for at least a day, the TV world's
latest entertainment. And tomorrow? A child

again. A dead child. And my friend, a child
himself really, puts down his blue
coffee mug and shuts his eyes. The world
goes on, my friend, I say. Can't soothe the pain
of everyone. I know, he says, the map
once more of childhood—oh the papers

I could write on the caring child who papers
over need by being needed, the child
of alcoholics who can't move on. Your map

is more than that, I say. Your dear blue
eyes betray your warmth. He turns. His pain
smokes and curls to silence. And my world

stops. Why go on and on when his world's
dead to mine? On little scraps of paper,
wings that only briefly lift the pain,
I write like parents who recall the child
who's grown and gone as a boy in blue
jeans, smiling. Philosophy's off the map,

I say... But the map's unchanged. The world
on paper's all blue ocean, islands,
and two children with bucket, spade and sand.

Wendy Klein

Just Jacaranda

The colour makes you gasp,
and knowing you can't describe it; that words
are too usual: that bloody *purest blossom blue* –
the best Steve Tilston could manage –
or maybe just admit it makes you hyperventilate;
or consider the concept of ocular orgasm,
coarse, but compelling, or think of the Hebrew: *tehelet,*
the silk thread woven into your grandfather's unused
prayer shawl, though in Buenos Aires the locals claim
it's able to whistle Tango tunes on demand,
and when you see it dressed up in its Christmas skirts,
pirouetting down the streets of Adelaide to Tchaikovsky
in unimaginable, unutterable, brazen, dauntless blue,
you stop trying to give it a name, remember the way
that naming implies possession -- birth to death –
and you, above all, across continents and seas
where snow bends branches 'til they weep and snap,
cannot possess it; but only the link you make
to your childhood when you first saw its glory, before
blossom carpeted the ground, before you were left
with green silence, tracery of fern, naked foliage;
like the time your grandfather or someone said,
it blooms in places where old Jews go to die.

The people of Sahel remember rain

Less the lack of it, more the lack of the memory of it:
of children who had known only bleached–bone earth,

had heard only stories of it, told by grown-ups who shushed
them to sleep while they slipped into the night to drum

and dance it: the way it would steal from the sky, gather speed,
shimmer like silver needles, the way it would feel on the face,

the hands, its patter; how it could carve creeks on dust-covered
backs, on legs and arms that cracked with the lack of it,

and mouths pinch-parched, thirst unslaked by the slick of it
left in their great clay pots; so when it arrived one night

on tiptoe, a rustle of wonder spread from hut to hut, a rumour
like rat steps in corn, and as the first drops fell, fierce and fresh;

the pots began to fill, the river to rise, though in the noise
and mystery, the blaze and rumble of the sky, no one knew

whether to dance or pray—whether their gods were pleased
or angry; children and elders stretched out arms, cupped hands.

Richard Leach

Salt Air and the Seal

It's early Thursday morning
I am off for my 3 ½ mile bike ride
Along the coast through the marina
Then on to the beach
I am enjoying the cruise
Soaking up the surroundings
And the sounds of the harbor
Always different - it's beautiful
It's like an island oasis detached from the city noise
Amidst the clanging and the construction always going on
In this working port harbor town

On my journey - I spot a seal
Sitting very tall and upright
Basking in the sun and taking it all in
As he sits on the break water right next to the sail boats
That are moored near by

I made my way closer to the seal
To get a closer look
I heard this sound
So that's what the seal was listening to!
I could not believe my ears
I was simply amassed and I think the seal was as well

Jazz trumpet at the marina!
It sounded a bit like early Miles Davis or Clifford Brown
Or perhaps Don Cherry or Ornette Colman
Or a little stretching and outside cadences like LA trumpeter
   Al Aarons

At first I thought it was someone living on board one of the sail
    boats
Practicing his trumpet getting ready for the next gig
Sounding better than most- experimental in spots- yet cool

As I worked my way closer to the boats for further investigation –
    that was it!
That's what the seal and I were listening to
The sound of the metal wheel of the boat ramp the rising with tide
    rocking back and forth
Creating the movement and thrust on the ramp the pressure and
    flexing of the wood
The metal and all the elements coming together. Creating music!
What a groove! It was a moment that the seal and I will not soon
    forget.
Funny what the salt air can do.

How Many Nights?

How many nights did it take to get there?
The one nighters
Schlepping all that gear
Looking for service elevators
Back doors, side doors
Even trying to get past many closed doors

How many times did you have to ask
The club owner for the check
Only to have him say:
Come back Tuesday
We didn't do that much business
Even though the place was packed

How many hours
How many years
Did it take to learn your craft?
To get good - real good
To make it all fit
To rehearse the band
To take it out of your living room
Past your garage
To some make shift sound stage

How many auditions
Showcases, demo sessions
Backing up some want to be singer
Just so the band could have a gig to play

How many nights did you wonder
If you made a smart career choice

Or if anyone at all was going to come
And hear you play

How many times did you play
For one half of the door
Only to ask what happened to your half
You are the bandleader
With a minor degree in psychology,
Marriage counseling, not your own of course
Mediations and child development
How many nights did it take to get there?

How many tours were canceled?
Checks that bounced
Fights that you broke up
Times you were slapped in the face
And the car broke down
And all of the Motel Sixes you stayed at
How many broken promises
That were forever broken and unmendable

How many drugs
One night stands
Lousy PA systems
Busted amps
Unplayable guitars
And non-playing drummers
Have you gone through?
Your life is like a never ending
Set of lyrics and changes

It is your life, your dream
And your passion
Don't stop now

You have too many nights invested
How many nights will it take to get there?
I will have to ask you later
I know that you have two more
Shows to do

Marie C Lecrivain

Bain Marie

In Maria P's soul kitchen, it sits on the back of the stove next to the teapot, to be employed on the following occasions: holidays and cross-quarters, weddings and funerals, and emergencies like when the heart is broken. This is the time to put yourself in the capable hands of Madame Maria P. She will make you tea and read you stories from the *Book of Life,* while your heart, enclosed in copper and stainless steel, simmers in aqua vitae. When your heart is healed, it will be carefully placed and sewn back into your chest with the admonition: *When you join the male with the female, you'll find nothing but trouble.*

Opal

Laugh. Be clever. Work the crowd back and forth
until you're sweating, and your right hand aches
from all that waving. Look, you've dimmed the North
Star's splendor. You've proved you've got what it takes
to outmatch the misery, and hold back
the darkness. It can't touch you, so long as
you remain upright and no one sees the crack
in your armor. Don't forget; the show has
to end sometime. The mummers need to be paid
and the audience wants to go home. Sad,
isn't it, to be alone with your frayed
nerves and uncertain future? You'd be mad
to think this is the end. Alas, not so.
Everywhere you are—and no place to go.

Suzanne Lummis

When In Doubt Have a Man Come Though the Door with a Gun in His Hand

Raymond Chandler via Lawrence Raab

I'm in doubt, all right, let's
lock the door, dear, lest
a gun come through in a hand

attached to some punk,
some goofball declaring it's all
the fault of society. Or is it

you who comes through the door
shouting gibberish, how I
doubted your word,

how I pretended but never believed…
"Lies! Lies!" The syllable yelps
make me think of a man detached

from his ski party calling
for help, but now I'm not sure
who cried "Lies!" I had thought

it was you, but then why
am I framed in this doorway, this
stunned .22 in my hand

weeping a curl of smoke?
And who was it again I just
blasted straight out of this fiction,

this construct of lies? Dear,
if you're still here fetch me
some aspirin and a stiff drink,

I have a headache. It's not
the suspense that's killing me,
it's that existential doubt—

I got those unreality blues.
If only I could arrange
for the right man to come

through the door with a gun…or,
no, not a gun…a fruit
and cheese basket, singing

telegram? A package stuffed
with hard cash, laundered
and pressed with an iron?

I'm certain only of the door.
Yes, there is always
a door, in fairy tales the portal

to a different world. But here
its "knock knock" is the set-up
of an old joke, or the question

that might turn out to be loaded.
Or, like the sound of one
conferring with oneself, it might

just echo back
Who's there?

The Night Life Is For You

Here, on the boulevard of run-
amuck dreams, each stamped
with a doll-like face you half-
recognize as yours, the neon
displays its chilly, self-
possessed light.
But the lips on the billboards
are raspberry cream. They say
Buy me or Be me, you
can't tell. You're confused
like mad again, in this night
of mixed blessings spiked
with a ripe curse, that line
you fall for every time.
You'll drive these streets
in a trance after your death
crying I'm still here!
but now you get out and walk.
This pale, feverish presence
inside your life is you,
and those are loud strangers
gripping beers. But why die,
ever, while stores shout out
their bargains, hot CD's,
and one can gaze at the bodies
who've stopped dancing now
and stand about jaggedly
because the doorways
of rock clubs pumped them
into open air? No doubt about it,
all of this is for you.
Some Doo Wop tune

on the airwaves says the night's
thousand shifting eyes
are on the watch. You guess
two of them are yours.
Tonight Mr. Good
or Bad might pluck you
from the crowd.
There's some place you're
supposed to be, some fun
you're supposed to have.
It's fate, your fate, and it's open
twenty-four hours.

Rick Lupert

In Piazza San Marco

Dueling classical outfits
cause the tourists to run back and forth

across the square to their different renditions of
New York, New York

We take seats based solely on proximity
pay the *Ten Euro Music fee*

Addie has mint tea and I order
water with bubbles, my Italian favorite

We spend money in Europe
like we're making a movie

We have the best seats in the house and our quartet
is rounded out by a piano and an accordion

Listening to classical music in Europe
is like growing a baby from a human being tree

The violinist's bow is frayed
They're taking a break now

My water gets less bubbly
with each passing empire

At the Tel

When you get to the place an hour early
everything becomes something to look at.

The sea of couches, the highlighter
left behind by the woman who swore

on her life it wasn't her highlighter
The guns in boxes out of reach

proving everything, when displayed in a box,
becomes art instead of the thing it was meant for.

A door opens and no one closes it
until the self-appointed *Captain of the Door*

gets up and closes it, and just before,
a voice drifts in from outside, just one phrase

I like trolls. And I'm so glad powerful statements
are still being made. Did I mention the sea of

couches? Samuel L. Jackson staring at
a pole of descending faux vines. At least

that's what he wants me to think he's looking at.
For Christ's sake whose highlighter is this?

What kind of world is this where people
leave highlighters strewn about and refuse to

claim ownership of them? In the bathroom
graffiti, above the toilet, about eight tenths

of the way to the ceiling, says *dangerous bros rule*.
I'm at the 'Tel, Redondo Beach, where *dangerous* bros rule,

where a man made of metal whose guts
left him centuries ago keeps us all safe,

where I couldn't grab a decorative gun if
I tried. The sea of couches...

The unclaimed highlighter...
The poetry is coming.

Sarah Maclay

For You Who Are Not With Me Who Are With Me

Because you are such a cloth man, I must start with the cloth
report—in this case with our friend in gauzy white on black, those
famous black grapes dripping from her earlobes, dangling in
strands, as she assembles the seating, checking out the room,
while our thin and vibrant friend, in a green frock-that-could-be-
called-a-frock, jokes about her reading glasses as she reads to us—
all smoke and leaves and wood and sex and shining and the Seine
and dusk and our friend/her friend whose mother died and father
died and husband left and son is leaving for college and who is
sparkling now in the awkward embrace of a life she does not
know, in green, in jeans, more fully alive, and our friend all reds
and oranges and peach and freckle-diaphanous-lit on her two
martinis and cackling, eyes jade olives, penetrating, vividly, the
air, and her friend/my friend with the pulled-back hair and the
dozen brothers or so and tonight her friend in specs and our friend
whose husband also left four years ago, her graying hair now
shoulder-length as though she's been allowed to become a girl
again as she smiles with her new and bearded, twinkling friend
and his grown son, and our other friend who loves our (not here)
other friend but it was over a year ago or two and she's pulled
together in a chic-er lace brigade (if not brocade) and her hair, all
auburn-toned, allows her to wear her body differently, somehow,
with a kind of now-found stateliness and *her* friend (who I've only
recently met) is champagne, all joy and frazz—and now, as I turn
to the back, our blond friend who I'd imagined sitting next to
tonight while gazing at you in a mini-skirt, no stockings—only
instead I'm wearing something I didn't need to iron—a blousy film
of longish dress with flecks of fallish flowers, all brown and longer
and black and under it the stockings covered from bottom to top
with flowers, brown and orange, gold, that some have mistaken in

the past, in airports, for tattoos—but you see I can take them off and wash them—and so (this is where we went tonight) our red-haired friend is making me walk across the room while lifting my dress and it's only at the end of the evening that our blond-haired friend moves closer, breaking into tears because of a migraine so I manage to cadge a couple of Advil from our friend with the grapes and after sausage and a beer our blond-haired friend is nearly glamorous again—a word I shouldn't use, you know, but will—tossing back her head with the friendly guy in the leather jacket and glasses who's always smiling, and also with my tall and sylvan friend (*she* slips two folded paper sonnets into my drawstring bag but later, when I tease the black silk open there are only a couple of pieces of antique lace) and her husband—while below, a crowd of hundreds jams into the outdoor brick café, twirling scarves and almost dancing, every age, to hear a young guitarist twanging out her evening chords and beginning to sing and of course—to go back to the room for a second—our friend who is playing the saxophone (though it's been nearly confiscated as a weapon and someone says it was because of the case—it looked like a gun—but no, our black grape friend says, no, it was the instrument itself that set off rumors)—and his forehead, tonight, just beginning to bead with sweat, his wrists embraced, encircled with, on one, a sleek *très* Western watch, on the other a necklace of brown and wooden beads, from Africa, I think, but do not know, and tonight he is the firmest of brown mountains blowing into the lacquered sax—its brass keys set on top of a horn so silvery it's almost black and the sound that pours from it is gold and silver and black and black gold and it hits my neck now, which is where you come in—as my head begins to drop on its hinge and I close my eyes and my hair, already frowsy, dangles like limp cloth and it's all a river now, of our accidents and multiple and singular desires and words and leaves and smoke and dusk and the Seine, all shining, and then the way your hand, right now, descent under water, would have given itself to my neck and the way I would, descent,

135

go under, anywhere with, under flame, with you, even as the high brick walls in back of the terrace, where I'd imagined leaving the crowd with you and leaning into—even as these walls, this turf is guarded by security, in white—and all the secluded benches are taken and even the long, oval pond that is really a fountain reflects the night like a slippery stretch of patent leather, like the most alluring couch, so that I have to dip my hand in now, so that I have to break the surface with my finger—ok, the merest trespass—and *actually*—and let me slide that word around in my mouth and taste it—let me fondle it, if I must live with it—the way it starts with an opening and gets complex in the middle and leaves my tongue with another kind of opening and even though this is not the night we'd hoped for, it is all of this and actually this—*this* is what we've made.

At the Thrift Shop Café

I don't know how many times I've passed this
   grove of yellow Hawaiian shirts
      (as if people wore them once
        and sold them back to the store—
        they always look the same
        and there are so many)
and taken this very corner into the back of the store
   where you can actually eat,
      but today, as I'm about to join my party,
      I'm stopped by one item of clothing—
        and it's a shirt I once bought my ex-husband,
        which he tired of, and gave to me
      but which happened to fit my now ex-lover,
though I see he's put it on consignment—
   it hangs on the rack with four or five
      other brown shirts
        I sort of recognize
        near our table,
   where my ex-husband and my ex-lover sit,
   commiserating,
really nearly weeping—
   and not even about me,
      but about their careers—
        and of course I'm wearing red and black
        (but not my own:
   the clothes belong to one of them—
   I'm not sure which—or both)
and the waitress complains:
      if we're going to eat in her restaurant,
        at least we can show her the courtesy
        of wearing our own clothes.

Ellyn Maybe

He Kisses Girls Just 'Cause They're Blond

He kisses girls just cause
  they're blond
  because he knows I have brown hair.

Another kisses girls just cause
  they're blond
  because he's considered
  an outlaw in his culture.

Another kisses girls just cause
  they're blond
  because it will make
  his father jealous.

Another kisses girls just cause
  they're blond
  because she wants to start over.

Another kisses girls just cause
  they're blond
  because T.V. told him
  that would make him happy.

Another kisses girls just cause
  they're blond
  because he says the desperation
  in their eyes is so loud
  he becomes wet.

Another kisses girls just cause
    they're blond
    because he's overweight
    and this makes him feel thin.

Sometimes I feel sorry for blond girls
    as I stand alone
    and kiss myself.

Someday Our Peace Will Come

one day poetry dropped from the sky
and the animals grew iambic pentameter tails
and the people breathed in stars

one day music dropped from the sky
and the architecture turned symphonic
and the people breathed in harmony

one day memory dropped from the sky
and the past present and future sifted like flour
and the people breathed in wonder

smoke and ash
as distant as two sides of the same coin

Julianna McCarthy

Ars Poetica

"If your father ever saw the filth you wrote he'd break your leg."

—*Sr. M. Emaline, ssj*

She stood, an axe of a woman wrapped in perpetual mourning, waving
a note she had captured. My note to Mary Dolores Weir about
Saturday night back-seat calisthenics with a boy from Cathedral Prep.
The note that, mercifully, did not make it to my father. It did,
however, keep me after school, leading to my missing my bus home,
leading to my mother having to come and get me, leading
to my banishment to my bedroom where, limbs intact, I was free to write
all the filth I could imagine.

The Fall

With the gates about to close, the Cherubim waiting
impatient and imperious, Eve went to tell the bees
that she was leaving. Went to tell the orchard hives
the trees they swept bore fruit unlike all others, fruit
so rich her eyes were opened to the sweetness of fear,
the bitterness of time.
                              Uncertain now of Paradise,
unwilling to loose this new-made woman, the bees rose up
around her, ready to dance the way out. As she led all flying
creatures, and Adam, all the animals – even the serpent
wound a path behind her into the Autumn of the world,
leaving Eden empty of everything save Judgment.

Terry McCarty

Ode to the Sylmar Bear

at least two local TV news crews
harsh light of LAPD helicopter
fish and game employees on the ground
a tree comes into view
easy to climb
but no branches
and not enough room to sit
on top of the dozen or so palm fronds

so it's time to reverse course
find a front yard to be cornered in
and prepare for the sting of the darts
plus premature hibernation
before waking in familiar surroundings
glad to be free
from those who couldn't relate

One Small Step

I took a compliment today
instead of returning it
like an undersized sweater
resisted the temptation to say:
glad you liked my poem
but so-and-so wouldn't
instead, I drank the glass
filled with accolade
it tasted like the purest water
enabling me to relax
and enjoy the rest of the day
without allowing so-and-so
to be a phantom companion
uttering hypothetical negativities,
causing me no end of worry

Elaine Mintzer

Catfish

In this chapter, I'm a catfish sliding through muck, trailing my Dalí
barbels, swallowing everything.

Above me, carp fan their golden tails and nibble mosquitoes
hatching on the surface.

Above them, a bright eye that traverses the blue.
A dim eye that follows the black.

At the bottom, we theorize about life above the surface.
We've heard it will be like this:

A last meal.

A pierced cheek.

A line that draws us out of the depths, into the lethal air,
its absence of pressure.

The blinding light.

A many-limbed creature, grasping a long antenna or
whisker.

Its eyes gleaming at our introduction as it removes the
hook,
for which I am grateful.

It is rumored that afterward I will be cut—tail to throat—to the
    bone.
What is after?

On the Evening News

And that's the way it is."
——Walter Cronkite

Over dinner, Dad waved a chicken leg
above the squad of canned peas on his plate.
He lectured about the need for military might
and accused me of condoning anarchy:
My protesters, *my* hippies, *my* long-haired freaks
tearing the fabric of society.

Mom stood at the kitchen sink, her back to us.
We never glanced at the crooked bow of her apron,
at a widening run that laddered up her calf.
And she added nothing to our argument
as she scrubbed scorch from the Revere Ware.

On the evening news we heard the fracturing
of America: troops and enemy killed,
rioters beaten back with tear gas and billy clubs,
demonstrations and disorder.

At the table, the war.

On the TV, the war.

In our house, a ripping
that would, years later, remain
cemented in our family.

A rift that took decades to heal.
That remains sensitive to the touch.

Michelle Mitchell-Foust

Exponential

Never enough quiet for saying *logarithms*
are the opposite of exponential functions,
not enough to say *sunflower,* remembering
the crisp corpse of one delivered to me anonymously,
from someone who knew so very well the significance
of the spiral of its seeds that I kept it for years.
I was trying to say *radioactive decay*
inside the dull seashell roar of class.
I was trying to say *the time of death of a bear,*
which I calculated once when I was young.

Logos, word rhythm, I see the absurdity
of the numbers shifting, even as someone,
not for the first time, points out the window
to the pigeons below us on the basketball court.
The room gets quiet. I stop everything and watch
along with everyone else. A white bird
with two black spots looks so much
like a Holstein among the other grey birds
that some of the girls name the bird *Cow.*

Three days we see *Cow,* and guess at its origins.
Here at this school where everyone is cousin
to everyone, this white bird may just be a dove,
because doves and pigeons are cousins,

and do I have the heart to tell them that the white pigeon's
perception of time is logarithmic, that given the choice
among short or medium or long flashes of light,
the bird will be the best at the long flashes,

his good guesses bunching up at that end of the graph:
his skills, in this world at least, exponential.

If Anything

for Christian

I.

They have a rooster in the apartments
behind the geometry room, two hanging
cages of birds, a pair of doves in one,
and nothing in the other, and the odd square
cut high up in the building, maybe for the fuses,
but it's gushing a dry dark straw and power wire,
a pigeon nest abandoned. The rooster, autonomous,
as he glistens and floats up the stairs.

Maybe loss is why I dreamed the red-tailed hawk.
It was simple, the bird flying down to where I was,
on the other side of the glass, and we, a mystery someone
and I, watched the bird shiver and swell and circle himself around
so his hint of red fully blossomed and he grew whiter
where he was white, redder where he was red,

and he stayed there with me, inches from my hand.
A woman I tell this dream to says a red-tailed hawk
means intuition and seeing things from above,
and the window I saw the bird through is about transition,
and the red underside of this massive puffed-up beast
signifies creation. After the dream, the rooster disappeared.

II.

Maybe this is why I dreamed about my best friend
and a little movie I made in the dream a year
after she passed away. She didn't recognize me
in the film. She kept saying the names of people

I don't know. This was my second or third
dream of us sliding between pews.

The cloudbank is separating horizontally at one end
into inelegant parallel lines that simply end, each line
ending at the same place, so that vertically, the clouds
look parted by hand. I'm relieved when I hear
the rooster crow after his silence. He crows, flapping
on the hood of the blue Nissan Sentra every morning after this.

III.

Maybe the bird's homecoming is why I dreamed
myself singing a song I didn't know, or maybe
one that didn't exist, singing it in a field,
or I was walking around a field singing
with another woman's voice: with the held-out notes
on *love* and *strong*. I didn't know anyone
in the dream, and I was teaching people to sing in a field,
seeing what happens when sunbeams
come into a building, lighting its shadows,

the Brownian movement being a host of miniscules
mingling, and the bodies least removed from
the impetus of atoms experience invisible little blows,
so we can see them with our eyes. Like the rainbow
I conjured in the canyon. I could see its beginning
lighting a tower on the mountain. Maybe this good omen
is why I dreamed a quadratic variation of a martingale,
a steadying fastening, a doubling down after every loss.
A particle, in this case a rooster, starts from the stairs,
feels the random disturbance at right angles to the path
of the soapy hand of a child, the water spray off a van
outside in the alley. The child forces the rooster to sit,

holds a flamin' hot Cheeto to its beak, and it eats
before the bird chases three girls in pink shirts out
from under the carport. We are too far away to smell
the bird and the burning smell of a bird's chest.
A boy I know folds a hundred-dollar bill
into a thunderbird to show me that the trees
make a wisp of smoke. See, SEE, he says.
He says I know something. I'm just not saying.
Wait, he yells, still folding,
Wait! I can hear your heart beating.

Bill Mohr

"And the warm weather is holding…"

We watch foreign movies, in the sweltering hours before us at
  midnight
Knowing that even more weariness is in store for us at midnight.

If I think this is hot, with no oasis before us at midnight,
Imagine the past tense of loneliness joining our chorus at
  midnight.

The temperature is literal, embalming humidity,
The metaphor that turns everything porous at midnight.

No matter how implausible their gratuitous jealousy,
It's impossible to ignore past lovers who implore us at midnight.

You learn how the familiar—a paved, two-lane road—
Quickly becomes terrifying to walk, if in a forest at midnight.

Be forewarned: tantalizing ecstasy must be set aside
As infantilized reverie meant to allure us at midnight.

Someone else, it's consoling to know, is enfolding
The consecration permitted to the aurora borealis at midnight.

Maybe if you imagine a million other voices, Bill, each pitch
  perfect,
You could glow like a providential constellation near Taurus at
  midnight.

Ghazal to Accompany Old Age

The slightest gust of soothing touch can mend, with language,
The graveled path, embanked with snow, one comprehends with
    language.

Side room book shelves circumference with language;
My bedroom nightstands' binding bends with language!

I now accept that I will never read any of these books
A seventh time; they linger with an affection I suspend with
    language.

I'd rather spend the afternoon gazing at their slivered mosaic,
A spectrograph of intermingled contraband with language.

Backward, in my own days, I see the acid trippers
And parsimonious linguists foolishly contend with language.

Some people choose Jesus or vacations with exotic winds,
But I have no better lover than a silent friend with language.

Open to any page, Bill, start with the first cathartic word,
And let the ripeness of this instant blend with language.

Raundi Moore-Kondo

God Bless Us Everyone

Bells of freedom ring
and wake me from
my three worst nightmares.

I am not chained to this bed.
I throw back the curtains
and call down to a boy in the street
to ask him what day it is.

He proclaims "It is the morning
our saving grace is born!"

Which means:
I am not too late,
YOU are not dead
and I need not be alone.

Crippled and small
as you are,
I have let go of the coins clenched in my fist
just to hold up your head.

As I dress for our cooked goose,
I will sing from this windowsill
of my love for you
and this world.

I want everyone to hear
though no one will care much.
I owe the world a good laugh

after all that crying
and pitiful whining
and pining I've done.

My song will always be sung
at the top of my lungs,
out of key,
on purpose,
so you will recognize me.

Let's Get Out of Here

If we decide to hike, the weather will surely turn
torrential and deadly.
If we decide to take a short cut, we will get lost
and will never be seen, again.
If we take the scenic route, we won't survive the photos.
If we go by sea, we will drown
If we go by air, we will fall to our deaths screaming like banshees.
If we wear parachutes, we will only become tangled in the lines
and fall to our deaths screaming like tangled banshees.
If we are carried off by long toothed predators
back to their nests, we will be torn limb from limb
and eaten alive by their hunger-pained young.
Unless, we are dropped and fall to our deaths, first.
Then we will be eaten after we are found dead.
If we eat before we leave, we will be poisoned
If we rest before we leave, we will be attacked
in our sleep by savages or damned in our dreams
to a life of crime
If we slip out the back, we will most likely slip
into quicksand, or else
we will be ambushed and scalped.
If we hide in the bushes in the backyard,
we will be killed by killer bees
or struck by lightning.
If we stay here,
we are trapped and as good as dead—
No matter what we do,
this story ends badly.

But, if we can get back to the porch
before the streetlights come on
we might just be okay, for tonight.

Jim Natal

Moses

> *"...the blonde*
> *and blue-eyed bringer of truth, who will not easily be forgiven."*
> ——B.H. Fairchild

My father told me this story just once, rare for him....
Away at college, Depression-era Virginia. The days
when he wore suits to class and the dogwood
and azaleas bloomed. It was a Friday night
and he was playing poker on the Sabbath.
Fraternity brothers, beer and white lightning, also
a stranger who kept staring at my father
over the spread fan of cards in his hand. Finally,
my father had enough of the stranger's eyes.
An athlete then, fit and handsome,
he called the stranger's bluff, called him
out, put his cards face up on the table
and challenged,
What are you staring at?
Did the boy——these were college boys, don't forget——
blink or abruptly stand, the others at the table
perhaps catching the first scent of rain
in the air before the storm arrives? When the boy
responded, his words were whittled
from tones of the purest, deepest south.
Are you a Jew? the southern boy asked. Asked.
My father said he was. The boy spoke again.
But, he said,
you don't have any horns.
The way my father told it, he did not
hit the boy, though he wanted to. The reason
he didn't fight, my father said, was because
158

the boy was serious, incredulous, shaken. All his life
this boy had been told that Jews
had horns, like Michelangelo's marble Moses.
And now, face-to-face with his first Jew
in the flesh, the Jew had nothing
on his head, not even a yarmulke. My father
stopped his story there, did not
describe the other boy or mention if he ever
saw him again. Was he dirty
blonde and lanky, Adam's apple protruding
from a banded collar, shoulders braced by
suspenders? No, that would be a stereotype.
Was the boy the first from his family to ascend
to college, a good possibility then. And what,
I wonder, did the southern boy do that night
after the game broke up and the stone
became his? Did he brood on the mountain,
carry the weight forever in silence, a holy rage
repressed? Or did he take it down to his people,
go home and topple the idol, this boy
of gold now fallen himself? And I,
in my own college haze, did not think
to ask my father,
Why are you telling me this?
Why now?
Never expecting that it would be
the first and only time.

Rock, Earth, Wood

What I remember most about my father's funeral
is not my young daughter's first dance
with the angel of death,
or the steep slope of the cemetery hillside,
the heat of the day,
my mother's lost tears,
or the dark knot of my father's friends,
black against the parched green,
chanting the Kaddish that mother and I still
stumble through standing at his marble marker,
her spot beside him already paid.

What I remember most about my father's funeral
is the sound of my shovelful of earth,
sucked dry, pocked with rocks,
as it hit the wood of his coffin, and the force
in my throw, how I seethed
overturning that heavy spade,
and how my anger embarrassed me
as the others who followed,
more experienced, perhaps, in the etiquette
bent low and made their contributions
with gentleness, love, respect.

And I wonder, was I angry at my father
for leaving, at the Lord for taking him
before I was ready to let him go, at myself
for allowing him to die without saying goodbye
because I was too late that early morning
and he was not strong enough to wait,
the hospital room I entered now filled
shovel by shovel from the mounded grief

beside his open grave and me digging, digging,
hearing that sound when I see the telephone
and I reach...

Keith Niles

The waves of sadness

The waves of sadness sweep in lately and take me out, all
foundations to earth wash away and I whelm over with the
sadness of this world. I am overcome lately, the waves wash
through and all is lost, all foundation to humanity is gone,
my tether snaps, my emotions possess me, my shoes filled
with mulch, guts, my heart a heavy sponge the waves of
sandess sweeps sandness sandness over me, and eyes
swimming in the tragedy of the death of the whales.

Sometimes lately the battlements of years break and the
water comes rushing through and I am caught, and
everything else was a lie, a front, an anger born of pain, a
painting a show that I was not born to play in. Sometimes it
all breaks, sometimes there's just nothing I can say or do,
sometimes I have to let the ocean flow through me and hope
that everything will be okay at the end, forlorn that all has
been for naught, that none of it is going to work out after all,
and my soul has to leave this body and flow into the world
universe sea.

My boat sails out beyond the breaks the waves beat me
about the prow, I go under, I'm swept out and there's
nothing I can do about it, the sound of the gulls breaking
is o unbearably tragic, I drown.

we angelenos

we angelenos we creatures of an indeterminate age we vampires in the desert we the sages of sallow we with the pages of nothings we vampires with umbrellas we angelenos we angels we swimming the shallows we pictures of health we rembrandts of bar napkins we slumming the sours we with the sisters in the suburbs with the sons in the army we the betrayers our black wings splayed over the summer we angels we singers of sweet sin we without fathers we with the blood of vegans dripping off our fangs we angelenos we feeling our way forward with sonar we celebrities of stage and dream we tending to the cattle that throng to our cages we lean angels scanning eternal the desert the pyramids the sand we saints keeping slaves in the valley we with secret silos of water and the abs of deities we etching hieroglyphics of sperm on the pages we of the undetermined fates we shark skulls we duct tape we devils we daisies we dead we angelenos we angels we angels of an indeterminate age

Kim Noriega

Mermaid

The wind didn't still. The birds didn't hush. The lilies didn't
turn their heads. The mother's minted lemonade didn't spill
to the deck in a sparkling cascade.

I saw her little body sink, her chubby fingers flutter
like tentacles of a miniature pink anemone, a few wisps
of strawberry hair waving:

Good-bye, good-bye.

It took seconds. I slid into the water, scooped her up and out
of the pool to her now frantic mother's arms. I was nine
years old. Afterward, despite the sun's warmth, I sat, shivering,

at the edge. The way her eyes had looked—wide open, beckoning.
Two sapphire oceans I could have seamlessly slipped into
                              —stayed a mermaid there, forever.

Name Me

The power of naming is two-fold: naming defines the quality and value of that which is named—and it also denies reality and value to that which is never named, never uttered. That which has no name is rendered mute and invisible: powerless to claim its own existence ... this has been the situation of women in our world.

—B. Dubois, from *Convicted Survivors: The Imprisonment of Battered Women Who Kill* by Elizabeth Ann Dermody Leonard

Name me the girl
with the slate-blue eyes,
the girl who sits under the apple tree,
your apple-cheeked bride.

Name me your lover—

the mother of your eight-pound baby boy.

Name me *sugar lips.*
Name me *honey-girl.*
Name me *sweet potato pie.*

Name me the woman
with the black and blue eye.

Name me white roses.
Name me *I swear baby.*

Name me crushed larynx.
Name me fractured mandible.

Name me *but I was high baby;*
it don't count when you're high.

Name me *whore.*
Name me *get in that fuckin' kitchen,*
bitch.

Name me dislocated shoulder.
Name me *what ya gonna do,*
have me arrested?

Name me *I dare you*
to try and leave me.

Name me the woman
with seven broken toes.

Name me the *cunt*
you tell not to make
a sound.

Name me *tramp, slut, ugly*
ball and chain.

Name me the woman you love

to get up against the wall
and fuck with your .38.

Name me the woman
who found the dog
lying in a pool of blood
outside our daughter's door.

Name me the one who dug
the dog's grave; posted *lost* signs
the next day with our kids.

Name me the mother of children
who will never be safe.

Name me sleepless.
Name me *the little missus*
who bought a 9 millimeter.

Name me *shows no remorse,*
name me *guilty as charged.*

Name me not sorry.

Name me widow.
Name me the woman in cell C-15.

Name me free.

Judith Pacht

Spider

she hangs

between
    drywall & cement
    floor & painted wall
    inside her tangled mess

resting
    belly up & naked
    private parts
        exposed

her crimson birthmark
calls out
her name

I wonder if she's weary
    her day filled
    spinning
            fetching a silk taste
                a fly-by
caught in a cycle   spinning

            me
                I scoop lint
                from the dryer   weather
                strip a leaky window

            quotidian comforts
                kill what's precious

both of us
                    intimate assassins
        spinning

to cover
            death's dark cheek
            his scratch & stubble

                    the ink-black
                    deep in the iris of his eye

On Giving a Silver Fox Piece to Jessica
(which of course was rejected)

because
            no one
                wears real fur in school

because
            animal rights people stop you
                        & make rude comments

                                            do you blame
them

anyway
                    The *vulpes vulpes* coat
                    is glossy   warm
                    enough   to withstand
                    the wildest wind
                    even sideways sleet   cool
                    enough   a gift   of comfort
                    in a shaded thicket

            NOTE: The silver fox in the wild is monogamous.
                The fox's habits are typically cautious.

            droplets from a stream he fords
                        glisten
                        slide off his oiled pelt

                        Following each mating period
                        both parents raise their young.

        so who in conscience could wear real fur

& besides   I

don't have anything it goes with

although   around the neck it does flatter

Candace Pearson

Lili St. Cyr's, Hollywood

> "Not another bombshell,
> but a real atom smasher."
> —Dorothy Barresi, *Glass Dress*

Peer through the dusty windows into the shop
overflowing with faint promise in satin and silk,
and there – see, in the far aisle, you can't miss her –

my younger self, blushing as she ducks behind
a rack of French maid costumes, this girl for whom
sex/love entwine, all lure and hook and catch.

Take pity on her, offer her a booster shot
of human kindness. Best not to ask too many
questions about why she's come,

just imagine a man waiting or simply
unsuspecting: she will try this hard to sway him.
Not the only way she knows,

but the only surety. Choices bubble and vamp:
which fandango, which boy, any boy?
There's the formal maid in high starched collar

or the short-shorts with strategic cutouts, then
the slits, the tassels, the feathers, blameless maribou
shrewdly positioned. Two elderly shopkeepers,

between them they've guided a century
of French maids: *Oh honey, won't she look cute in that?*
Oh yes, oh sweetie, it's smashing, it's you, as the girl
172

holds up a hanky of backless black satin with
rhinestone studs, ready to bombshell her way
into someone's beating heart for a minute or two.

Coffee Break

A doctor on the radio warns
there are 37 known toxins in a coffee bean,
unless you buy organic and even then,
it's not a good idea. That devil caffeine.

Kona, Columbian, Sumatran, double-roasted,
free trade. I celebrate you – the perfume
of another last chance, of an empty highway
and full tank at 2 am, a new beginning
in every hot swallow.

In the Ardennes, in northeast France,
ten cups of coffee are taken after dinner, each cup
possessing its own special name. My favorite: *Gloria*.
As in worship, religion, obsession.

My mother can't remember her own name anymore.
Or how the parts of the coffeemaker
fit together. I watch her in her kitchen, forcing them
the way a child tries to shove a block circle
into a square.

On her back porch, jumble of plastic and glass,
derelict graveyard of coffeemakers.
Damn coffee people, she tells me,
nobody makes quality anymore.

In her old life, at the elementary school, she was known
for her brewing skills. *Let Mildred make the coffee*,
the other teachers would say. *Let Mildred.*
Each letter of her name drip, drip, dripping
into the pot.

Cece Peri

The White Chicken Gives a First Hand Account

from an Associated Press Story

I love the red
wheelbarrow
rusting
by the barn—
my sturdy
nesting place,
my refuge
the night
raccoons
laid waste
the coop,
killed all
the laying hens
but me.

Farmer
buried them
in the far yard,
and Laslo,
the brown dog,
dug them
back up,
nuzzled each
gray bundle
against the long
hen house
and, there,

all morning
stood guard.

Laslo,
brother of my heart.

Trouble Down the Road

At the flat top grill, he was all business,
flung raw eggs dead center into the corned beef
hash like a strapping southpaw.

In the alley, with me, he was all ideas.
Said he'd be leaving soon, had a shot back east—
a tryout for the big leagues.

Said his sister would loan him a Buick convertible,
and he'd fill it with malt beer and tuna.
All he needed was a woman to hold

his cat while he drove.
I like animals, I told him. Then I dropped
my cigarette into the dusty clay,

ground it out, slow,
felt the road under my foot.

Penny Perry

501 Valley Drive

for John

Chaste in our pajamas,
we held each other
in that knotty pine bedroom
until our wedding in TJ.

Back in our bungalow
on Valley Drive,
after vows.
me, slipping out of my wool dress.
Your skin, smelling of salt water
and lime cologne,
saving me.

Morning coffee, your Marlboros.
Palm tree in a lumpy patio.
We sat under the rusted umbrella.
Your dark blue eyes
matching the cotton of your shirt,
the dark blue ink of your pen
in your long tan fingers
filling out the racing forms.

Horses galloping us
out of our future

After Midnight

Tapping. Sometimes I think I still hear
her footsteps, the resigned tread
of the insomniac. Two weeks now.
Peach branches outside my bedroom window.
The clock on the living room mantel strikes three.
I've laid out my school clothes, homework.
Maybe it is the wind pounding on the front door.
I slip on my white robe, the last gift my mother
gave me, hurry down the hall.
Clatters, crashes in the dining room. I flick
on the chandelier. Tudor window panes shudder
and break. A creature with broad shoulders
is climbing through the black space
where the window used to be.
I pick up the dining room chair, the one with
the lavender pansy my mother hooked.
I think she will be mad if I break her chair,
then remember she is dead.
The creature had cleared the window now,
flung itself over the love seat.
"A man's home is supposed to be his castle."
My father stands in front of me naked.
I try not to stare at the red, pubic hair,
his shriveled penis tipped jauntily to one side
as if trying to wave. I have only seen my cousin
Rhonda naked in her bubble bath, and Mrs. Robins,
Linda's mother who after cocktails stepped
into her above ground plastic Dough boy swimming
pool, her floury floppy breasts heading straight
toward my face. "Why the hell did you lock
the front door?" he asks. I can't see where
blood dripping on the rug is coming from.

I set the chair down between us.
Something smells yeasty like freshly baked bread.
His breath is a cloud of Jim Bean.
"Where are your clothes?" I ask. "Somewhere,"
he says. "Your keys?" I peer
into the night. "The car?" "Somewhere else,
God damn it." We stare at each other.
Although it is spring in Southern California
ice seems to be rising from the floor,
through my toes, up my legs and calves.

He turns. Trails of blood run down
his clawed back. I picture a woman's red
beauty salon nails. Glass shimmers on the love seat,
on the rug. Our ordinary dining room
where my mother served her meat loafs,
 her pot roasts, now glitters like the ballroom
at a palace. The king of his castle, white buttocks
glowing, marches down the hall. Over his shoulder
he says, "I'm going to bed. Turn off those lights.
You'll run up the bill."

Bren Petrakos

School

His grandma walks with a hobble, her house coat is black with a sparkling blue flower pattern, she wears it proud as they walk to school.

On her head is a blue scarf, clean and pulled tight over her almost white curled hair.

He loves her brown eyes and fat hand, he loves the little home made cookies she put in his Superman lunch box, and the way she smiles when she wakes him up in the morning.

When the other boys at school say something about the way she looks and walks, there is a moment.

What he does with this information in that six year old moment, is important, how he processes the tease will determine his everything.

He looks away, sad, then mad, then he closes his eyes and remembers...She loves him "bigger then the sun, bigger then the moon and always!" So, with fury he turns to the boys, and shouts

"Go away! You mean nothing to me!!"

It is the birth of a free man

Rainbow

I didn't know it,
But there is a rainbow in my closet
under all the stuff
Wanting to be its transparent miracle
Wanting to be promise
Waiting for the storm to settle
the old world to be moved

I knew a boy once
He wanted hope to be sent like a dove
into the air
finding land
Bringing a branch of peace
he whispers to me from time to time
There is hope
no matter what
no matter what
its how I found the rainbow today
in the closet
under the stuff
mixed with the whisper
no matter what

Darby Power

love letter to everything I am and someday will be

ATTENTION

I AM HERE TO CHANGE THE WORLD

and sometimes I like to smoke a cigarette
even though it's killing the planet and probably me too.

I AM HERE TO CHANGE THE
WORLD,

And fuck you for thinking that this right here
Is anything other than earth-shattering.
My bullshit poems may overflow
with optimism and beautiful girls
and the way a certain sound
always reminds me of midnight,
but that doesn't mean I'm not working
on bringing the world to its knees.
That doesn't mean I'm not shouting the truth
to the heavens on high
'til my voice goes hoarse from listening so hard.

I AM HERE

on a lost energy high and I'm waiting to crash
and drinking in the adrenaline until I do.
    I kiss with my teeth.
    I feed on the air.
    I break all my clocks

because time is for the lonely
and I'm learning to keep company in my back pocket
for the moments I'm alone with my thoughts.
There isn't time for anything else but honest today,
and tomorrow I might hate myself again
so for now fall in love with the pieces I scatter
across receipts and old road maps
I never learned how to read.

THIS LIFE IS A ROAD MAP

traffic will fuck you over no matter how many back roads you
    take
you will always have to buy gas eventually
you will get lost
there is nothing wrong with asking directions
there is *nothing* wrong with asking directions.
The directions you get will often be wrong.

But you will get where you're going eventually,
although Foster's concept of the quest
tells us the destination
is never where we're really headed. So

I AM HERE TO CHANGE THE WORLD,

but maybe instead I'll eat a hot dog
or a really good salad,
maybe I'll never learn to drive and instead
roller-skate backwards with my sister's ukulele
and learn to speak Klingon
and dump regret in the junk drawer
with broken earrings and waterlogged matches.

So far, I've learned to spell love
seven different ways,
and my favorite doesn't return my calls anymore,
but then no one does anything but text today anyways.
You will never know
what my first thought was today,
what my last thought was when I was eight, and
maybe that means that you'll never really know me.
I've never been one for dramatics, but

THIS IS THE END OF THE WORLD

or maybe the beginning
and fuck you, anyway,
for building pedestals too tall for me to climb.
I've never dyed my hair and I've never smoked weed,
but people are dying and sometimes I think
it's somehow my fault,
the way hummingbird wings lose their life
when they stop for too long.
I'm barely nineteen, but what if I'm still
too long stopped?

I am here, to change the world.
And it has to be okay.
Even if I make nothing more amazing
than dust
and notebooks full of ink stains.

WE ARE NOT GOING TO DIE

today.

Retrospective

One,
you don't believe in quickly-written love poems,
so I wrote you one,
quickly,
because *I* believe in *you*
and the impossible
and the way the writing you down makes me smile,
and because I'm writing this on a day
we both believe in ourselves.

Two.
I forget to try to look my best
when I'm with you.
I forget to be anything but me,
and happy,
and occasionally breathless

Three,
I spelled *occasionally* wrong just now
and I think you would like that,
and I like that I think about things you would like
even when you're not here.

Four.
I don't write good poems
about falling in love
and I know that and try to avoid it
but somehow
I've written three about you already this week
and I don't even like two of them
but God, they're making me smile,

Five,
you make me smile,

Six,
I make you smile sometimes, too.

Seven.
Time works different when you're with me.
In that it isn't there, mostly,
it forgets to exist
when it's just me and you.

Eight,
sometimes I think my old poems are about you
even when we hadn't yet met.
You're important enough
to have found a home within my past,
the way the best friends are the ones
you feel like you knew years before you really did.

Nine,
I forget I'm supposed to pay attention to other things
when we're together,
so forgive me the times
I will continue to trip over sidewalk edges
because I've been looking at you.

Ten,
this isn't about you.

I mean it is, but mostly it's about me
and the way I fall for people
quickly
and repeatedly,

and it's never once worked out,
but I'm still a romantic
because
people like you
are worth being a romantic
for.

Eleven.
People like you
are why
I *do*
believe in scribbled-down love poems,
in the words that flow out quickly,
before we have time to regret
all the love overflowing within us,
and how happy it feels
to write it all down.

Twelve,
I was going
to stop at eleven,
but I want you to know
that you're worth one more.

Marilyn N. Robertson

The Dark Side of the Moon

Started out in Wyoming where coyotes
howl, rustle you out from your bunk.
Out there, you learn pretty quick
how to respond to a threat.

In school, kids who thought
it was funny to come up
with rhymes for Cheyne soon
decided it wasn't that fun after all.

Got a taste of the Ivy Leagues.
Didn't take to it. Had a few
scrapes with the law. Now the law
bumps up against me.

A bum ticker sidelined my run.
.
Late at night, I stop at the window,
check the reflection. Like the dark
side of the moon, my pull extends
over the mountains, beyond the tides.

Still riding that same horse I came in on.

Coyotes

Show some respect—
they've been here long,
may well be here long after.

Adaptable, they eat
almost anything--note
all those "Missing Cat" signs

taped to telephone poles--
those cats, my friend,
are never coming back.

Related to the wolf, fox,
and jackal, they can mate
with dogs, a rarity

though people would turn
and point at our dog, Tim,
saying, "Oh My God!"

Active when sunlight wanes,
they yip and howl; by day
they vanish,

the color of dry brush
their numbers rising in Los Angeles,
present but unseen,

like the rest of us, from big towns
and small, anonymous here
the way we like it.

Beth Ruscio

Imaginary Memorial

Instead of a mausoleum, it's a performance art swimming pool.
Jerzy Grotowski wears a gilded tri-corn empanada on his head,

bronzer on his face.   Hair silvered and jet, he's vaguely
    Musketeer.
Kipping off the high diving board, he flubs a twisting dive,

water slaps all over.   If we all wore empanadas on our heads,
goes his theory, our identities would be established on sight:

diablo, dulce, jamon.   Fluent in Salsa Blanca, *I'm used to larger
    bodies of water,*
he says, smoothing back his bangs.   *Reservoirs, lakes—they're
    more my zone.*

Then, Dad and Mom glide in, that eight-thirty gait, all grace.
Both restored to buoyancy, though they haven't swum in years.

Late, as is their fashion, for the funeral.   *How did you get here?*
The hug goes on so long that everybody dives.

Ready for magic? says Mom, unusually amuseable.
One minute, she's pulling off evening gloves

the next, she's smoking and singing like Sinatra.
We took La Cienega   all   the   way

191

Non Grata

We lay in the dark, breathing together.
—Louise Glück, *Faithful and Virtuous Night*

An indigo North Dakota winter night,
enter a girl, in between abandoned and thorn,
dirty blonde ribbon in her hair, B.O., annoyed,
an ongoing annihilation with knit brow. No hello.
Not likable. Obliged to hear her rant, I really
tried to talk to the dear darkling. Nothing doing.
Oh, wow, tell me to go lie down and all day like garbage I rot.
A kid. Wary, daring, wayward. A tyrant.

By God, to be like that, a tangible knell,
world weary energy all day, a lethal will
to hit the terrible wall again, letting go
like a battered door in wind. Her wronged tale,
hardly grand, we're nothing alike, are we?
Yet I let her go on. Let her reign the night.

Cathie Sandstrom

Ferret

Fifty pence each. With wages saved from picking
strawberries, my son bought first a cage. The farmer
made him wait, visit several times, handle the
animals to be sure. *Y' must handle 'em often
to tame 'em. Still they'll bite. Best to wear gloves.*

In a shoebox tied to the back of his bike,
she rattled over the farm road between
Hutton Wandesley and Marston Lodge.
Theodora: cousin to mink and weasel, long
elegant body gleaming, her round head not
as pointed as rat or mouse; black shining eyes.

Over the summer she learned our hands, the kitchen
and scullery where she lived. Holding her felt like
trying to hold time…constant movement, all lean
muscle tensed to spring forward, away.

At Michaelmas in late September before
Fall term, my son took her cage beyond
the barn, released her into tall weeds
and nettles. An easy living for her there.

Weeks later, I felt the house settling back
into its old routine as I laid the fires, riddled
the range's grate to add more coal. Come in
with an armful of laundry stiff from the line,
I left the back door ajar. On my heels,
picking her way cautiously, Theodora,

like an expatriate Russian countess,
her coat nearly winter-white.

After a Siege

After two scorching weeks
in late September,
as after a war
I venture out
to assay the damage.

In the garden, something
has stripped the basil to sticks,
then started on the sorrel.
Doubtless a grasshopper,
mulch-colored marauder.

Vines sag. Tulip poplar's leaves,
crisp as corn flakes but more brittle,
blanket the pots below. Hard to tell—

Summer's lingering fire?
Or Fall? My kitchen window
interprets the leaves as coppery.
The siege, over. I want to drop
to my knees in gratitude

as when waking from
the dream where you
ask to come back and
relieved, I realize
you can't...you can't.

Gerard Sarnat

Election Day Get Out the Vote Yankee Doodle Candy

> *Jimmy can crack corn but I don't care*
> *My enemies crack corn but I don't care*
> *You can be black white or albino, yeah*
> > —from Eminem's "Jimmy Crack Corn"

Whilst dem ole demon massas begin
to die off like hophead blue-tail flies,
us nigga ex-junkies' newest grandsons
make dat doormat slumlord apt. dormant
hickory pony cart an' sunnyside ups come
alive homey—but whetha Trump or Hillary
theys ain't 'xactly our own Barack's cornrows
so we don't need no honky weathamen to know
which way the wind blows poor folk once agin.

trouble among the lovely loving Hmong

black slate
hill country
above Laos
& Thailand

plugged into
glam rock band
Black Slade.
a blank slate

cold but not
quite so high
froggies boil
in thin air

—except for
perseveration
about ant colonies
= brains stitching

tribal leaders
exit hot tubs on
technicolor rills
below foggy peaks

neurons together
into wisdom
+ rumours her
Ford Mustang

to wrangle/ auction
hundreds of wild
calico ponies middle
of god-knows

convertible was
vandalized by
inside jobs near
Goa or Delhi

which's where
my under or over-
medicated shorn
companion who

+ overheard
family quarrels
taking place in
a distant room—

may be in need of
more intervention
than one drug
holiday is

she recalls nada
as we fly home
early 'cause I
can't bear more

Diana Sieker

Heart Insomnia

Once your heart wakes up,
It can't go back to sleep.
At first, it stays up all night,
Watching in horror,
The humans who create
Hell on Earth
Through endless war and hate.
But, over time, it strengthens
Through use,
Like exercising a muscle,
Until it is fully capable
Of loving
Even those who are asleep.

[Untitled]

Crack open the hard shell of your heart like a walnut,
And let all the pieces crumble completely,
Only to be swept up and brushed away neatly,
Like a floor rife with peanut shells after a circus,
Cleansed so discreetly.
God bless the world's circus custodians—
Those who choose the behind-the-scenes over the podiums—
For there is no job more spiritual than cleaning up after
The absurdly senseless extravaganza
Of ego and vanity,
Of spectacle and insanity,
When the three-ring circus of humanity comes to a close.
For those who can engender sincere smiles and laughter
Without wearing a ridiculous ball on their nose.
For those who know that after any level of enlightenment
You still chop wood and carry water,
While the rest of the world
Sits back to imbibe the mayhem and slaughter,
Distracted from the one thing that will keep them from their woes.
And as for the lion tamers, there's no greater danger
Than the beast inside their minds,
But the ego is actually the tiniest monkey
On the tiniest bicycle
On the tiniest of tightropes
On the loneliest of rides.
You think you're the ring master calling the cues
But there is only one performer to master;
Only one part you should choose:
And that's YOU—
The true self that resides in your soft naked heart.
The walls will be excavated and broken apart
In order to see the beauty and power within,

So pull back the closed curtain, and the show can begin.
Walls around hearts were meant to be broken,
Just as the stars were all meant to shine.
The ego believes that the magic only happens in the limelight,
When the truth is it happens all of the time.

Linda Singer

Mythology

I sit on a telephone wire.
while crows create the world
with shiny found things;
while sparrows fight for nests
chasing hawks away.
The line dips with my weight,
propels me into the open sky.
I land in a barren peach tree,
the fruit fallen to the ground
bruised yet untouched.
I conjure smoldering dreams,
of pleasure and sanction and consent.
I hoard happiness in closets, on shelves,
hang it from the backs of doors.
I am not the world creating crow,
I will not escort souls to the land of the dead,
I will not fall from this tree,
I will not rot on the ground,
I am mortal, wingless.
My face yellow ochre,
I will dance on eagle's bones
an earthly resurrection.
I will open my arms, not to fly,
but to embrace another,
I am made of passion and mud,
to hold, to hold, to love.

Anxiety

Problems perch over entrance ways
to fall on my head,
to implant seeds of doubt
into my weak and battered brain.

Problems swim like alligators
in the bubble bath of my life
to clamp their sharpened teeth
into my legs and pull me under.

Problems hide like antifreeze
in my Kool Aid to blind my mind's eye,
to leave me too crippled and afraid
to walk the treacherous way home.

Problems sneak up behind me,
like Freddie Krueger, grab me by the
tender throat with steel claws
choking the breath from my body.

Problems cloud my sunny days
with iced bullets aimed
at the windshield of my dreams
to slow me from my no destination.

Like the backyard German Shepherd,
staked to its laundry-line-leash,
to run circles in the neglectful
neighbor's yard,

One day, I will pull off the collar,
rip my neck free of the yoke,

face my problems down
with one fierce bark.

Graham Smith

[Untitled]

1.
in-n-out burger
for when bj's fails to give
full satisfaction

2.
jumbled wind voices
flood across the desert night
each with its own plight

3.
in every room
of our house
i feel his absence

4.
she works on her tan
as the summer breeze flips through pages
of her open book

Joan Jobe Smith

@ Naked Street & Reincarnation Way

If reincarnation is really real,
I do not wish to be reincarnated,
Tossed out into this cold world
Naked again. It's taken me all my
Life to find enough clothes to keep
My soul and skin warm and I
Still don't know what to wear.

Moonglow à Go-Go

Come on baby, it's June!
Dance me to the moon!
Light our fire, smite our dire while I swoon
seeing you in your blue suede shoes, white
sport coat and a pink carnation, me in my tight
tight red dress, high heel sneakers so we can go-
go shake rattle and roll, rock around the clock as
you drive your cherry-cherry pie Buick 69 fast
past Route 66, the yellow rose of Texas, gals in
Kalamazoo, Mississippi mud, New York, New York,
beyond the sea, smoke upon the water, blue heaven
and the twelfth of never somewhere over the rainbows.

Only you can love me tender, dance me where stardust
trombones moan us weightless as we sway sambas
cha-cha la bamba high and low-down in outer space with Mars
Saturn and Jupiter in our face, the stars a tiara prize
in my hair, moonglow a go-go in your devil moon eyes
as we fox trot a boogie-woogie wa-wa-wa-Watusi sighs
and do-wop and be-bop-a-lula like a sister Lucy.

Call me li'l' Darlin', kiss me once, kiss me twice my
60-minute man as saxes slap our backsides.

Waltz me in the Milly Way, far-out and out of sight
tango, dip me a total eclipse as our backbones slip
and you light my fire, smite my dire, kiss again my lips
begin the beguine dancing me, prancing me, enchanting me
crooning and spooning me April and May and June
with wings of angels on our shoes

all the way to

the moon

Wanda VanHoy Smith

Carnal Knowledge of a Tomato

I plant seeds in February,
visualize red ripe tomatoes by July.
Green sprouts push up and excite me.
The plants grow tall and spindly
with a few yellow blossoms
that shrivel and drop.
My friend's bush is fat and full,
heavy with golden blossoms
and emerald tomatoes.
When I complain about my
barren tomato plant,
She points a green finger at me
and says, "Your plans need propagating.
Are there any bees in your neighborhood?"
I shake my head, recall with guilt
spraying the bees in my yard
with something that froze them
because they had stung me in the face,
gave me lips like Julia Roberts for two days.
My gardener friend advised, "Touch the center of
each blossom with your finger."
So I go from blossom to blossom, touch
and hum, "Oh, What a Beautiful Morning,"
hope the tomato will mistake me for a
hummingbird.
With great satisfaction,
I watch a baby tomato form and grow.
Who thought I'd get a thrill from sex with a tomato.

Teddy Bears Don't Talk

I volunteer at the Good Samantha Thrift Shop
see nightmares hiding in the eyes of battered women.
The girl could have been twelve or twenty
standing with dignity on dirty bare feet
a baggy Bugs Bunny T shirt cannot hide woman's curves
silver braces cage small teeth
try to hold a trembling lower lip steady.
She holds out a voucher,
They sent me from the shelter for clothes."
Bright spring sky eyes wise and cold as winter avoid mine.
"Take what you need," I wave at pipe racks
sagging with near new designer clothes refugees from
crowded closets of career women.
I'm a fairy godmother with a wire coat hanger wand.
"I have lots of clothes at home," the girl woman says,
"If I go back there I might not be able to leave."
I nod, understanding that falling from cozy nest hurts
even when full of lice.
She comes out of the dressing room in a tight tank top
jeans make her hips look made of blue denim.
A man knocks over a rack of paperback novels.
She tries to disappear in a bulky sweater.
A child playing dress-up she puts on shiny black pumps
teeters on stiletto heels
a low filthy whistle makes her kick the shoes away
pull on high-top sneakers
shoes made to jump rope, bicycle ride and run.
We pass a shelf of toys
a cuddly bear holds out stuffed arms.
She stops, "I had a bear once. I told him all my secrets.
Dad threw him away. Said I was too old. Is twelve too old for
a Teddy bear?"
"How old are you now?"
"Fifteen."
I hand her the bear, "Tell this one new secrets."
She walks out the door wearing her new life
and holding her secrets close.

David St. John

Bumble Bee

It was such a Fifties kind of thing
The astonishing sport coat at the back
Of the drop-dead expensive Roman men's store
I'd passed by almost every day just off

The Corso & sure enough it was exactly
My size & it's almost impossible to describe
The vibrating sense of pleasure
The soft lines of alternating butter-&-black

Gave to the haze left in the eye of
The gazer in this case meaning me as I stood
Before the mirror
Smoothing the lapels along my swelling chest

& the woman beside me herself just a little
Breathless turned & said, "Oh honey, oh honey...."

The Opal Trees

When I awaken into the dream

Of your body upon my body
I am breathing the fragrant air of
The opal trees where shivering rags
Of light pearlesque the limbs of
Your body upon my body
As I awaken into the moonscape

Of this solitary bed
Still feeling the soft satin of stone
& the blossoms of the opal trees
Littering the sheets of earth beneath me
As their shattered rinds
Swirl through the branches of the dream

Of your body upon my body

Terry Stevenson

Godzilla

You giant radioactive lizard,
show biz legend for fifty years, some thirty movies,
lots of sweaty Japanese actors in rubber suits,
as a kid I marveled at your blinking dorsal spikes,
flashing moments before the blast of dragon breath
incinerated all in front of it.

Godzilla, your time has finally come –
a star on the Walk of Fame,
a few steps east of Grauman's Chinese Theater,
next to Tom Selleck.
Tourists from all over the world flock around
the pink-and-gray terrazzo pentacle.

Godzilla, like Cher, Madonna,
Prince or Beyoncé,
only one name is needed.
Godzilla, I want to crawl
into the magic costume,
let loose my inner reptile,
stomp Tokyo, torch the White House,
tear-up LA infrastructure,
punch a hole in Parker Center,
before the military puts me down,
thinking I'm gone, not knowing
I'm the closest immortal this side of God.

Reading the Warning

Do not drink wine from the temple cups,
such sacrilege will not go unnoticed.
I can read the writing on the wall
but maybe I should keep it to myself.
There is power in secrets.
I don't fear death
the crows may dine on my eyes
the wolves may eat my entrails
yet I am happy
for I have kissed the soft lips
of a woman about to be sacrificed,
a happy martyr to the good life:
white picket fences
two cars in every garage,
a chicken in every pot,
and the morning dew,
wet on the bright green lawn.

Kevin Patrick Sullivan

Blue Sky

There is something big as the sky inside you
A blue cloudless sky
An ocean inside you

Have you heard it move
Along the lines of your eyes
Felt it run the heart's valley
Crest its snowy peaks

Have you dreamed inside your waking
That sound so silent
You know you're not alone

There is something big as the sky inside you
A blue cloudless sky, an ocean
Inside you are the dreams
I look for in my waking
Inside you I know
I will meet myself

Sleepers

For Patti

Under the silkwood
Sky of night
We build
Inside each other
A new skin
Something to be
Out in the world
In

Paul Suntup

The Painter

Meg. Meg. Everything was about Meg.
A famous surrealist painter used her as
inspiration for a piece about solitude.

For her nose, he painted a cherry orchard;
her left cheek was a hive of wild geese.

Meg loved the attention. Every day at noon,
she would come to his studio and sit for the day.

"No makeup tomorrow please," he would say,
"I will be painting your eyes. And when I start
on the midnight orchestra of your body,
no clothes please."

On the twelfth day of her right leg,
the canvas, a tortured sea of blackbirds;
she cried watching him. "Stop it!" he yelled.
It's hard enough already."

"But it doesn't have to be this way," she said.

During the last week with her back turned,
he traced the curve of her spine in the air,
mixed seventeen colors on his palette
including Absolute Zero, Electric Ultramarine,
African Violet, Boysenberry and Dust Storm.

He painted an African hut between T4 and T5,
a herd of charging Wildebeest on the southern

border of L2. Then came the trees. White Ash,
Sugar Maple, Black Walnut, Black Birch, Black Ash.
Butternut, Eastern Hemlock, Sassafras, Black Cherry,
Black Willow, Sycamore, Scarlet Oak, Balsam Fir.

He left her arms for last. Her arms. Not clocks,
not a train, no men in suits, no trees, no birds.
A painting of a woman's arms. So clear and certain.

"Put the brush down," said the arms;
hands pressed against his bruised skin.
Fingers interlocking with his. "I am here,"
said the arms, "I have always been here."

Haystack

I drove to Ojai and stayed at a lodge.
There was murder in my room.
The wooden bed was full of murder.
It was drunk on murder cocktails.

Even the wooden walls were murderous and violent.
The rug had a PhD in murder.
The rug graduated at the top of its class
in Murderology.

There was violence and murder all over the room.
Great hulking haystacks of murder.
A museum filled with paintings of haystacks
in painted fields. All those brutish bailed stacks
of hay in all those painted fields.

Like thousands of slaughtered American buffalo
on the grasslands of old Wyoming.

I was too afraid to go in the shower that night.
I lay on the drunk bed on top of the covers
and slept in my clothes.
I didn't want to get murdered.

It was a cold night and I kept waking up
every hour or so. The murdered bodies
were tapping me on the shoulder.
Then when I fell asleep they waited
an hour before waking me again.

Getting back to sleep was not easy
with all those slaughtered buffalo staring at me

with their helpless eyes.

It was like bailing hay with broken fingers.
Morning came eventually and I got up
and out of there fast.

"Goodbye room," I said.

Even though it was a murderous night,
I felt sad leaving the room.

All that ancient wood and desperation.

I looked into the room before I left
with sadness in my heart.

I felt like we had shared a violent night
together and I realized I hadn't felt
so alive in years.

G. *Murray Thomas*

Charlie Brown in the Strip Club

He would not normally be in a place like this,
but the invitation—for a drink—from his coworkers was such a
    rarity
that he accepted without asking where they were going.

He tries to hide his embarrassment,
his eyes shifting nervously from the nakedness on stage
to his rapidly warming beer.

But when she walks on stage
his face turns as red as her hair,
and his companions can't help but notice.

He is so flummoxed he does not see
their heads bent in conspiracy,
the money counted out, and passed along.

Just—suddenly—there she is, writhing in his lap.
She doesn't seem to recognize him,
but did she ever even notice him, back then?

He knows that THIS was never what he wanted.
Nonetheless, his heart pounds, his skin sweats,
his hands hover mere inches from her still unattainable flesh.

"Your Kidney Just Arrived at LAX"

The doctor told me as I lay in pre-op prep.
I envisioned a special chartered flight,
an entire airplane filled with organs.

Hearts with little heart shaped carry-ons.
They always watch the inflight movie
and cry all the way through.

Livers splurging on one last drink;
they don't think they'll be allowed
where they're going.

The lungs eye the spot
where the oxygen masks drop.

Corneas stare out at the passing countryside;
they always get a window seat.

The spleens are always complaining
      about security
      about the length of the flight
      about the lack of leg room
      (although they have no legs).

The gall bladder always gets in line
before his row is called.

And there's my kidney,
no doubt reading a book to pass the time
something classic: A*s I Lay Dying,*
      or *Great Expectations,*
      or *The Stranger.*

All of them wondering
about the journey ahead,
about their new home,
about their new life.

Lynne Thompson

Siren

Eternally lured by calypso,
    Daddy wanted to return
        to his birthplace, to the Mighty Sparrow.

He knew about heat's seduction, about steel pans,
    maracas, about the Canboulay, all
        brewed in the Indies' crucible of revolution,

underpinning the peg box and scroll
    of a violin Daddy also favored—yes, Vivaldi!—
        who (his sons said) couldn't best Jellyroll

Morton and his hepcats blowing with the Nat King
    Cole Swingsters in every California beer joint
        until the money ran out; Sassy Vaughn singing

Black Coffee and Nice Work If You Can Get It.
    Daddy admitted Duke and Roach (with his Jazz
        in 3/4 Time) were superior to any minor minuet

but sometimes he had a hunger for a polonaise,
    a Schoenberg twelve-tone, a Bartók sonata that
        his daughter drowned out with Marvin Gaye's

Stubborn Kinda Fellow and Dizzy's latest platter.
    Still, Daddy reminded us to kiss the ground of Port
        o' Spain where stick fighting's clatter

gave way to fry pans and oil drums or
        anything that could shimmy up a rhythm and
                put a dip in the hip of a late-night worker

because that music had given birth to the flim-
        flam singers his children were calling musicians—
                men twisting their fingers so hard it seemed

they'd forgotten bamboo sticks, jawbones and
        Belafonte blowing into white America—Day-O!—
                and oh, we didn't have a clue about the Akan

or any other African tribe who handmade the first banjo,
        calabash, djembe, and the call of Zimbabwe's mbira,
                the siren luring our father back to his calypso.

Binding

Very little had been written on
the construction of bindings.
—Jill Magi, *Something Loose Could Fall*

Ask me—
      I will answer: *sea* (with its stony wetness
                             & far flung)

Ask *if*
      so I can answer: *myrrh* (as in our history:
                          ancient, quick kindling)

Or ask _____
      Perhaps I will   But only
                      Then again, or

ask me to forget the answer
      as in the way of snow-melt

                      or the hidden seam

of a book's binding.   Even when you don't ask,
      I will demur   as in the way of John Coltrane

Ask again,
      I will say   *you, Torment.*

Carine Topal

Of Man, Woman, Snake, Fruit

Was she testing for poison
when she said "Eat,"
fondling the sin in her hands,

or was it just
an apple. *Tapooach.*

The whole time it was
breathe, muscle, walk.

So he considered the shape
of her breast and reached

for the *tapooach,*
thinking: this is the only
Earth. *Adamáh.*

And he named himself
Adam. *Adám.*

First man of *adamáh,*
to have the fruit, seed

to pluck from the tree
of more than one apple.
Tapoochim—

traceable to the blossom
of all things.

And the whistle
of a thing
called bird. *Tzipoor.*

And the hiss and rattle of a thing
called *nachash,*

muscling its way.
Nearby.

The Favorite Poet, 1888

*after the oil painting by Sir Lawrence Alma-Tadema,
1836-1912*

Time is a chamber, a willow. No, more
tranquil than a willow. The sleeping eye
of a newborn. We do not even sing. We
read our favorite poets of the continent.
Behind us, squares of light rest on the
wall. The floor has a welcome chill that
marble gives in the unexpected heat of
April. The walls are lined with engraved
copper sheets. The bronze-colored
window, which is not a window one sees
through, but a window that swivels,
opens to reveal a girl angel out in the
garden, spreading her wings atop a Doric
column. It is a room of anticipation in
which the words *ballad, pledge,
privilege,* are whispered to a hush. A
century we only hear about or watch
from a postcard, as I am doing now,
telling you who we are and what we wish
we were. How did we know to dress
wearing the sheer spine of a dragonfly?
Wearing, what so long ago, conjured up
words like spells in a chamber, like a
chamber in a locket, like a locket on a
neck, like a neck long as the day, like a
day of this lost time, of these faces full of
light. And despite our youth, laughing
had not occurred to us.

Kathleen Tyler

beyond the burn line

after the fire, we ride
past grasses stiffened black
bone raw oak trunks

our guide halts in a meadow carpeted
with carrion, leather-stretched limbs, splayed clavicles,
rib cage clasping the ruined prayers of clouds

a girl slides from her pony,
lifts the tiny, perfect cranium
of an unborn lamb, coyote killed,
here, in the savaged field

cool, oh, cool, how cool the girl's mother croons

she pulls a dried leaf, braille-pricked,
from her daughter's hair, cows graze, undisturbed,
an army transport plane rumbles by
its trail a gauze scarf trembling
sorrow gone to ground

I prefer earth to the heavens
a horse to a car; when I die leave me
in the bone field alongside scattered hooves and skulls
palms open to sky, the scarlet wattles
of turkey vultures bobbing as they feast

Car Advertising Alligator Farm

Clamped to the front of a 1936 Chrysler sedan:
an embalmed alligator, upright, waxy belly
exposed, back legs spread and shackled, tail sawed
off, the stump curled into a metal brace. Its glass
eyes, amber, gold, fixed in the sockets so they
don't roll but stare past the car's bulging
lights at maracas strapped to each claw. Its jaws
are hinged open, as though it is singing. Long
after this car became obsolete, my brother and I
carried home a pail of baby alligators from a roadside
stand. We tipped it, chased gators across sandspurs
tawny in dry Bermuda grass of that distant
summer yard. I trapped one against the chain-link
fence, tiny jaws snapping, chased it over and over
until Daddy drove to the swamp and made us set
them loose among cypress stumps and purple
hyacinths because just that day he heard on
the radio about a boy falling into an alligator
pit at the Paradise Souvenir Shop and Alligator
Farm. A witness said the boy floated down,
hands unfolding slowly, revealing something tender
and secret in his palms. The boy eager, expectant,
in his white linen sailor suit, as if the meeting
with the gator was inevitable, something he had
always planned to do on a cloudless summer
morning. As if he knew one day he would be in
a poem about alligators. This strangeness he sacrificed
himself to, this appalling beauty.

Rolland Vasin (Vachine)

Heavy with Child

When your daughter tells you that she is pregnant,
the one you championed from the day she slid out.
That's got to be a very strange situation for you,
washed over with memory of what you felt like
when you revealed to me in our living room
that the bandage on your arm, from Cedars' doctor,
meant you were going to birth a human but you didn't
know what that meant, and either did I. Your mother
knew, and you know now, what she felt like, all those lost
nights, terrors for baby's survival. Wild dreams,
sorrows, roam the mindscape and your sweet little girl,
her Mary Janes long-since given to Salvation Army,
is on the same path you were, and there's nothing
you can do about it.

The Smallest Caskets Are the Heaviest
—Ernest Hemingway

Nobody can explain why a child has to die,
certainly G_D does not kill children, does she?
Or, do you mean to tell me that G_D drowned
the Syrian boy washed up on a beach? His parents
rendered powerless to fend of water's obstruction
of the justice of air. Is that what I'm to believe?
I don't care whose god you choose, gods just don't
take lives of the young. Lucille Clifton planned
to ask her god to explain the deaths of her two kids
because she was pissed they were taken from her.
I too pray, for a reason for the death of our unborn
first child, why mother's job description was tossed
into the dumpster along with our fetus. Dagger my
chest so I feel what mother felt, drain my eyes
into salt flats, deliver me the imperative to surrender
my life. Place a sorrow wafer onto my tongue
so I can whisper grief into my wife's ear. Infuse
in me a deity's tolerance when wife, long into her
recovery, has not even set water out for supper, yet.
She cross-knits by gold-dusted twilight, past the cusp
of Summer, Second-boy breathes slumber-songs,
cradled close to her on our covered weather porch.
Conestoga heritage and the endless prairie tugs
her breastbone. Door County memories drift easy
into Season's-end breeze. First-boy, hand-in-hand,
with his grandfather in plaid, rustle tinder-stalks
of their backyard cornfield. Drop a stitch at dusk,
loop back for soul retrieval, lantern dims for all
the babies who couldn't stay...

Fred Voss

We Count Too

There is nothing I like better
than to see the big overhead tin factory door thrown open
to the sun
as soon as the icy morning cold on the concrete floor has lifted
enough to bear at 6:30 or 8:30 or 11:52 am one of us
strides from his machine and grabs that door's handle and throws
    the door open with a bang
        like the Bastille
has just been stormed
or if
it is a really icy winter morning props the door open with a foot
    high block of wood
to let in
just a little blue sky
just a ray
of sun
sun
that has seen the great pyramids casting shadows across Egyptian
    sand
a man walking a tightrope across Niagara Falls Lindbergh
waving his hat in a tickertape parade down Broadway black bare
    chested Jack Johnson
moving like a tiger across a boxing ring toward the latest great
    white hope Jack Benny
pushing his hand into cement in front of Grauman's
Chinese
we've been hidden
for so long giving the best hours of our lives to worm screws
and gears and barrels full of steel chips

behind tin walls
mother father wife sons grandson never to see
machine handle we turn or engine lathe chuck we lift
never to hear one foreman scream
in our face or one razor-sharp cutter shatter in a block
of tool steel never
one picture of us in a paper or magazine never
one story on radio or television
to tell them who we are
as they see their thousandth photo of Brad Pitt's face while they
    stand
in supermarket line
just one
ray of sun is all we ask just one
ray of sun falling through that tin door onto our face our hands
    our backs
sun
that saw Jack Kennedy get shot Ludwig van Beethoven step out
of a Vienna coach to conduct his 9th Vincent Van Gogh stare
at a sunflower sun
to tell us yes we count
too.

Shakespeare's Hardhat

University lectern
to sheet metal workbench
Ophelia
floating down a stream to drown with a wreath of flowers
around her head
to Max
challenging me to a grip contest so he can try to wrestle me down
onto a greasy concrete floor
books
against my arm to razor-sharp steel blocks cradled
in my palms when I dropped
out of the UCLA Ph.D. program in English literature and first
    stepped
into a steel mill and stood before a machine full of oily gears
instead of students
waiting for me to explain Shakespeare to them
it would take me decades
to find the poetry in a toolbox with its drawers full of cutting taps
    and radius gauges
and micrometers Ray
feeling the side of the head of his machine with the palm of his
    hand until he knows
if a cutter chewing through steel will snap in front of his face
or not
the horn of a forklift the roll of a 10-ton overhead crane
the glow of a red-hot bar of steel the hoot
of Javier the double thumbs-up
of Earl after he shaves a round bar of brass until it shines bright
as the sun Ramone
singing a love song from the days when his grandfather carried a
    gun

in the Mexican revolution below the border as his cutter carves a
  hub
so a wheelchair can roll an old man
toward his last sunrise rays
of sun falling through a steel mill window onto the tool steel
  handles
of a lathe just as illuminating
as Hamlet's soliloquy sweat
rolling down a grinding wheel operator's back after 10 hours of
  work noble
as King Henry the 5th leading his army
into battle
poetry is everywhere
under my fingernails Jorge walking down the machine shop aisle
  like a Madrid bullfighter
entering the arena 71-year-old Al
sticking out his chin like Rocky Marciano and going on though his
  wife is just 2 months dead
and he has nothing left
but a machine and look
over there isn't that Shakespeare on a milling machine smiling as
  he puts on
his hardhat?

Pam Ward

the last buzz before death

people around me are dropping like flies
I don't know why
but its seems like folks right
and left have been dying.
Daddy's gone
two grandmas went
back to back.
My friend's mama
dropped dead last June.
Flies are a lot like death
the way they crave the sweet
the way they hoover over
what's been cooked.
Take Mr. Smitty up the street
he was this ol' timey
shit talking
Friday night wino
who lived in this flop
by the alley
hoodlums and crackheads
would crash at his house
front door was a regular swarm.
Stayed torn up
stayed red-faced
from midnight till noon
booze oozing out
of each overripe pore.
Stole a whole case of Jack
during the '92 riots
folks racing in while

the liquor store blazed
phone polls lit up
like great big Christmas trees
place was a regular hive.
I watched his barefooted swag
down our street coming back
One smashed by his toe
but he grinned and kept steppin'
singing jingle bell, jingle bell, jingle bell rock
face looked like he'd hit the Lotto.
Used to stop by my place
to chit chat and kill time
told me, "One day I'm buying you
a great big steak dinner.
"Yes sir ree," he would wink
between long juicy swigs
and huge gnats making love to his sleeve.
Now I wished that I did
that I wouldn't have waited
or worried so much
what the neighbors would think
seeing me in the seat
of his red jacked-up van.
He used to come real early
and watch me pull weeds.
"If you were my woman
you would never to do that."
He was sweet
and real old
but still Romeo fine
with his tomahawk nose
and high cheek bones dug deep
in some black backyard
barbecue skin.

I should have gone
took the chance
made that fool grin his
crazy-ass Wild Turkey smile.
Should have went
grabbed my keys
let the front screen door smack
should have laughed
and drank Scotch over
over grilled filet mignon
should have gone
let the neighborhood
buzz if they want
let them swarm
let their fleshy tongues
fester like maggots.
Should have looked dead at life
zeroed in on the moment
like a fly does your plate
when you're eating outside
like your arm
like your fist raised
and gripping the swatter.
Should have told the man yes
tasted steak in my mouth
while the day was still young
not this dry throated
thought of him gone.

Sunflower Seeds

for Marlene Pinnock
beaten by policeman next to the freeway

I stole a sunflower plant in front
of the police station today
a wild screaming yellow stalk
fighting a bed of angry weeds

I snatched it in broad daylight
yanked the root with my hand
grabbed it like it was already mine
carrying it boldly
carrying it like royalty
like a golden precious staff
or stick
or baton
like the kind slammed against Rodney's spine
I marched down the street
in a single lady parade
daring somebody to stop me

I took the sunflower home
and planted it in my yard
near the barely hanging on broccoli
near the sad and stripped searched beets
near the carrots that came out of nowhere
I buried it thinking about my son
and how he likes salty black & white seeds
and how his speeding ticket could've turned ugly
when we picked him up that night
if the officer wanted to trip

I buried the plant with some poems
that didn't amount to much
something about water-boarding
and Zimmerman whipping ass again
but my first thought when I saw it
was of the homeless lady, Marlene
laying in the freeway, flat on her back
weather-beaten and wilted
shielding fist after fist
getting stole on, getting pummeled,
right & left hooks to the jaw
sitting on her stomach
straddling her hips like a horse
hitting her over and over again
in the face!
like his uniform transformed him
like he was a King
trampling black women like dirt
like mud underneath his boot
I thought, this lady could be
my own mother, my sister or me!
So naturally when I saw that flower
I rescued it from the police
because sometimes you just have to
march up to power
sometimes you just have to
combat the weeds
sometimes you just have to
snatch back what's yours
        even if it's a just a flower
        or a rock in the street
        growing like a riot
        in the palm of your hand.

Charles Harper Webb

Bouba and Kiki

> *"In experiments, 98% of people selected the curvy*
> *shape as bouba, and the jagged one as kiki."*
> —"Bouba/Kiki Effect," Wikipedia

They never got along. Bouba:
    soft, relaxed, blobbing
        onto Kiki's side of the womb;
Kiki: bristling like a hedgehog.

Bouba: injured, but forgiving;
    Kiki: brandishing a spiky grudge.
        Bouba: fatty everybody mocked;
Kiki: explosion nobody came near.

"Classify countries as Bouba or Kiki,"
    Dr. Tuckenroll commands in Poly Sci.
        "Is your signature Bouba or Kiki?"
asks Ms Lungfish in Calligraphy.

Bouba's blubber swamped Camp Woolly-
    Worm's canoe; Kiki's spikes sank it.
        "Counter Kiki with Bouba,
Bouba with Kiki," counsels Master Wu.

Bouba likes everything. Kiki's
    standards soar so high, she's blue-
        blooded from lack of oxygen.
Dr. Y wants Bouba to express

her inner Kiki; he dies of glomerization.
      Dr. Z wants Kiki to express
         her inner Bouba; his corpse looks
like it ran afoul of a knife store.

Our Bouba who art in refried
      beans and cheese nachos.
         Our Kiki, who in Halloween candy
doth hide.

Princess Summer-Fall-Winter-Spring

What Serpentine producer snuck her past the censors
to corrupt the Peanut Gallery boys? Oh Princess
of the Tinka Tonka tribe, I loved you more than Dolores
at the swimming pool, Janey next door, or Bobbi Jo,

the best baseball player on my block. I loved
the beaded buckskin dress that couldn't hide your curvy
hips and thighs. I loved your black braids, your dark
eyes that shocked me through the new TV, smudged

by my lips. Indian girl with skin as pale as mine—
birds and butterflies flocked to your singing drum.
Native Royalty, whose name evoked School's Out /
Trick or Treat / Santa Claus / Home Run Derby—

daughter (I guessed) of Big Chief Thunderthud—
you dumped Howdy, and left me to stomp
the flowers I plucked for you, and shred
the blue-jay plume I'd saved to slide behind your ear.

Starring with Elvis in *Jailhouse Rock,* you helped
to crown him King before you married a loser
named *Lafayette* who, driving through Wyoming
(near where Tinka Tonkan warriors ruled?) hit a car

towing a trailer that sliced your car and you in two,
ten years before Jayne Mansfield lost half
of her head the same way. The stone that bears
your white-girl name, *Judy Tyler,* says you were 25.

Elvis skipped your funeral, wanting (his mother said)
to remember you alive. I would have gone.

But no one told me. And I was still ("Thank God," *my* mother would have said) too young to drive.

Hilda Weiss

Gimme Coffee

Doesn't matter if it's bitter.
Pour it out and take another.
Get us moving back and forth between the parking lots.
Keep us buying metal cars reflecting light.
We are all reflecting light,
absorbing and repelling,
like this cup of colored water
that buys us every morning.

Horse's Skull with Pink Rose

Georgia O'Keeffe
Oil on canvas, 1931

First, the white extremity of nose.
The skull, you see, holds more than brain,
holds tongueless, narrow jaw
and gaping sack of eye,
holds ears—there are none left,
and yet the case is there—
sharp, white bone—for all the scents.

Second, the rose—extravagance of pink.
Pinned, it seems, into the brain,
the petals interleave to catch or to create
a dream. From the borehole rises water;
this horse blossoms from its skull.

Third, the middle ground on which are laid
flower and beast together. What is
this? Cloth, fragment of cup,
dry lake, pale winter sky? A place
of so much lack, so clean,
it catches, like a basin, everything.

Cecilia Woloch

Lucifer, Full of Light

> *"Every angel is terrifying"*
> —Rilke, "First Elegy," *Duino Elegies*

And if I should pick out the good in you—
each shard of broken light, like glass
from the wreck of your beauty, and look at that—

or one golden afternoon when you hovered above me
in rapture, oh half god—

how would I bear to lift my hands,
how would I bear to close my eyes
and let you fall, and love be damned?

My Face

I thought I'd grow up to be a fish. Or a tree, or a piece of wind, like God. I thought I'd scrape against myself until my face became my face. I never thought I'd grow up to look like my mother, much as I craved her one pink dress, stuttered around in her high heeled shoes, tried to sing the songs she sang. Or like my father, with his shadow in his shadow, pockets, keys. I planted tulips upside down, thinking those flowers would bloom in hell, and that hell was deep inside the earth. I walked around when I was small and spit my name into my hands. I wanted everything to shine. But I was dark. And could not swim.

Sholeh Wolpé

The Chill

On the bed's edge,
that precipice of loneliness,
sleep withholds its grace.

He presses his groin to her ass,
his warm hands loving her breasts,
the hollow of her waist,
her shoulder's arching bones,

kisses the nape of her neck,
sinks his head in her hair like a man
who's seen the dark ghosts of fog.

She wants to trample
this pain, give him
the lions in her throat,
the swans in her groin,
these wolves in her hips,

but her skin cries no, her bones
won't budge, and her tongue refuses.

When he pulls away, cold air stirs,
awakens a chill that freezes
and rends their lives into
a thousand irretrievable shards.

The Prince

The night of the dance I wore
an ankle-length caftan, hiding
my body beneath its airy flow, flat
shoes not to be too tall,
and my roommate's lipstick,
brighter than orange juice.

He was a prince who could have picked
any of the boarding-school girls—
Suzie with one eye blue,
full-breasted Victoria,
or the girl from India with a waist
slender as a drumstick tree.

But the sixteen-year-old Saudi royal
asked me for the first dance, then the second,
then for the rest of the night, as boys and girls
disappeared into dark corners while
chaperones dozed off in the hall
nipping Hennessy from tiny silver flasks.

My prince was shy, but not too shy
to slowly drop his hand and squeeze,
his lips on mine, the knife
in his pocket on my groin.

On the ride back the girls taunted me,
Camel driver's virgin, imitated my accent
singing, Don't touch the merchandise,
mocked me for pushing away the fetching prince
so hard he fell on his ass and twisted his wrist.

What did he do? Stick his finger up your...?
That night I packed my bag, slipped out
just as the sun exhaled its first breath into night,
took the first Eastbourne rail to London.
I hid beneath a beat-up hat, collar pulled up,
and by the time the headmaster was informed,
called the police and my anxious parents overseas,
I was at my clueless cousin's boarding house nibbling
baklava, drinking hot tea from a chipped cup.

I shivered beside a coin-operated heater, ate
fish and chips on yesterday's newspaper, and read
Neruda, Farrokhzad, for a week, Tolstoy, and Austen.
Quietly I thanked my father for giving me time
to strengthen the sinew that held my heart.

It rained and I didn't go out, avoided my big-boned
cousin with her roto-rooter tongue and the nose
of our grandmother who could smell anything
rotting inside the heart. I turned the cracked mirror
in my room towards the wall. Someone
had scribbled "HELP" on the back.

The rose-splattered wallpaper looked scrubbed
with day-old coffee. The lone sofa sagged
with the weight of absent occupants the way
my lips still felt the heaviness of that first kiss.

In the end what mattered, I learned,
were the smallest blessings:
the milk-sweetened tea or the miracle
of scalding water from the ancient bathtub faucet.
What counted were my widowed cousin
holding her own in a foreign land,

and the grit to say no
to what is hurled—words, glances, bullets, all.

Nancy Lynée Woo

The Rescue

A hound dog howls
by the side of the road.
I used to know that song,
wishing loudly for a peopled fire
and biscuits, soft touch.
Tail wagging as I approach
with my gun, I realize
those long dying days are done.
I call him into the bed of my truck,
feed him scraps of sorrow
until we're both full.

At home, the medicine cabinet
is nearly empty and pups
are due soon. The sky blooms
after storm and a hot plate
waits in a cozy kitchen. Out back,
the bloodhound sniffs at dandelions,
back leg scratching, paws busy with bone.
But as I watch, leaning from window
in between load of dish and towel
in his eyes do I spy a glimmer,
a slight murmur and pause,
do I catch him remembering
the long dark he came from?

Good Darkness

as in, penumbral moon
　　opening a silver
　　　　portal to

selenite spinning
　　　　words to questions
　　　　　　you

are trying to reach—but
　　　　not trying as in
　　　　　　ploughing

as in, fishing
　　　　on a cold, still sea
　　　　　　　—the moment

the reel catches you
　　　　straighten the line
　　　　　　　and become

the light

Tim Xonnelly

Carl wants to take me up on it seven years later and cockeyed drunk

driveway gravel at the window how romantic
on a Thursday is it really that late
but no it's just Carl wanting a floor to crash or a 20 til
next week or both

but he is on my neck when I let him up panting I love you
you know I love you
I push him off like a puppy like a big puppy
I love you too Carl but you fuck girls remember

he is pan in a panic his eyes two shattered mirrors
fourteen years bad luck his breath
twenty acres of dead grapes one hand now
in my sweatpants rolling my fuzzy dice like the

practiced seducer he is
I must be firm in as out you know you're drunk right
if you come back tomorrow we'll do this
and see him to the door

yes I did for many years want you Carl
but knew that that tomorrow would never show

These Are My Dumb Socks

I'm dancing with the yellow plastic
danger tape, floating in the parade.
I'm sipping a beer in a chaise
lounge dangling over the side of
the fourth story. I'm doing
somersaults in a tidal wave,
walking on the freeway. I
accidentally gave these
birds the power of speech.

Brenda Yates

Possibilities

Mostly the bodies were stiff and cold—
white-crowned sparrows, nuthatches,
chickadees—dotting the snow outside

glass walls they'd flown into.
Sometimes we felt a pulse as it quivered,
and ran to Mr. Wagner, warming stunned

bird with cupped hands and breath.
Removing his glove, he took it in his big
hand, rested a fingertip on the tiny breast.

We pressed in close as he decided, a long
moment like a fold in time.

Usually he squeezed, stopping the heart
before he threw it into a paper bag of casualties.

Now and then, he'd pause, pronounce
a possibility, and motion for a cage,
which then joined our classroom menagerie:

terrariums of snakes, frogs, fish tanks
and caged birds. There, the survivor revived,
chest hammering, feathers stirring as though

caught in cross-winds, or refused to eat
and slumped into a downy ball of no substance.

We learned about concussions, healing,
and that unseen element in the space between.

Animal-flower ABC's

Anemones belie
carnivorous design,
effecting flowery genus,
hiding in jaded knotty
languor. Marks never
observe predators' quick
reach. Sudden tentacle,
until very woozy,
xerotic, yes, zombie.

James Ysidro

Mathemoetics #1

Let X = the number of times you've tried and failed. Let Y = the number of sighs leveled in your direction. Divide by the interest accumulated over 7 years of marriage. Or lack thereof. Raise to the power of 2, sometimes 3. Multiply by the totaled future consolations to accrue from friends and relatives. Take a long walk. Make certain all the intersecting triangles still sum to 180. Consider separate vacations.

Mathemoetics #2

Let X = the very last night as a child that you watched the moon follow your car home. Let Y = the first kiss you took that left you more aroused than nervous. Let Z = the latest funeral you've had to attend. Sum these up between the parentheticals of the next full moon and the most recent meteor shower you couldn't be bothered to notice. Divide by all the things you ever pretended to love that actually left you cold. Demonstrate how zero became greater than or equal to infinity sometime in your early 20's. And why each new shot of whiskey now leads in a convergent series to the next. Prove that God is not just another Fibonacci sequence running through your head.

Mariano Zaro

The Actor

Once in a while, he comes to see me in the dorm.
He comes unannounced. He sits on top of my desk
with his back against the window.
Can I smoke? he asks. I sit on the bed.
It's a small bed, not comfortable.
I had to put a wood plank under the mattress;
it was too soft. I couldn't sleep.
I still cannot sleep; but it's not because of the mattress.

In the room there is a humble sink, a small mirror,
a glass shelf attached to the wall with rusty brackets.
On the shelf: toothpaste, shaving cream,
nail clippers. There is also a small plant,
a succulent that my sister gave me the day I left home.
This plant is indestructible, she told me.
But I know that it will die with me in this room;
like many other things.

I have dropped all my classes, he says.
I want to be an actor.
The sun hits his hair, and the hair is wheat,
flames, summer.
He opens the window, lights a cigarette;
keeps the hand outside.

I am going to the Avignon Theater Festival.
Would you like to come? he asks.
I don't know what to say. Avignon is far away.
I have no money. Avignon is for other people.

He turns toward the window,
looks at his reflection in the glass
and messes up his hair.
His profile is less impeccable now, less insulting.

It's getting dark. Under his thin cotton sweater,
his bony shoulders become harder, menacing.
There is no beauty without danger, they say.

He crosses his legs, knees almost touching
the Latin dictionary, my class notes,
and my journal where his name appears
in the same sentence, woven with other words—
grass, impossible, blond, balsamic, *azul* and magnolia.

Taxi Driver

He tells me that his wife is pregnant,
he just learned about it.

He is the taxi driver,
I am the passenger.

This happens at five in the morning,
in a taxi, on my way to the Madrid airport.

The taxi driver is young, handsome,
probably as handsome as he will ever be.
He is going home after this ride, he says.
He cannot wait.

Everything has a higher purpose now,
I suppose;
the way he stops at traffic lights,
the way he rolls up the window.

He drives through the city—
Cibeles, Recoletos, Castellana—
and the city turns and collects cells, tissue,
cartilage, bones, lungs for this child.
Madrid is the big spinning wheel
of embryos and invagination.

It happened so fast, he says.
We did not know it was going to be so fast.

I want to ask him if he knew
exactly when the conception happened.
If he felt anything different,

a stronger pulse, almost painful,
in that region between anus and
scrotum, in that equinox of flesh.

I don't ask anything,
I don't think is appropriate.
So I say the things you say in these occasions:
Congratulations, all the best to you and your wife.
I watch him driving his smooth drive,
the one I will never drive.

When we arrive to the airport,
he helps me with my luggage and I thank him.
I pay, give him a tip. Suddenly he hugs me.
Have a good trip, he says.

I can't tell if he knows what I am thinking,
what I want from him.

Felice Zoota-Lucero

I am a Cascading Waterfall

Pressure builds and it beats. Doesn't POP. Salt drips and it beats.
Doesn't STOP. I'm falling over a *WATERFALL*. I am a cascading
WATERFALL ricocheting down a creviced and serrated rock
WALL trying to not BLEED. I hold my chest *WALL* and apply
pressure to put pressure on the pressure to get away and stop
stalking ME, stop undressing my daily WORRY, barely allowing
me to BREATHE. My body explodes with an intenSITY while a hot
flash attempts to radiate my ANXIETY. I don't like hot flashes.

Sometimes sometimes sometimes, sometimes I spin like a gerbil
on a spinning wheel that is loudly silent screaming screaming
screaming, screaming silently about it *ALL*. I rewind the *SCORE* to
CRAWL in between treble and bass melodies and intertwined
harmonies as I fight with my recent stories reminiscent of a beer
bottle bashing bar room *BRAWL*.

Look...I know I'm not SLEEPING but I still see myself DREAMING.
I just can't rewind this WEEPING as it KEEPS SEEPING from my
PORES pouring out into the *WORLD* where I'm *VULNERABLE*. I
want to be *INVISIBLE* but too much *RESIDUAL* where I yearn to
be *IN SYNCH WITH YOU* yet *DISTINCT FROM YOU*...far from
invisible. I don't know how to be silent. I don't know how to be
silent.

So I tell my story...my words bounce through the air, radiate, and
then calmly tickle my toes as if I just took 3 long drags from my
wooden pipe. I'm falling over that same WATERFALL. I am that
same cascading WATERFALL but now it flows in slow motion
emptying in a peaceful translucent STREAM. I just need to take
pause and allow myself to DREAM with my eyes wide open.

It all started on a staircase

It all started on a staircase.

Sitting like a MEDITATING CONTEMPLATIVE Buddha criss-CROSS appleSAUCE at the top of my childhood scratchy mustard-colored STAIRS hugging...no...wrapping my little arms around Mr. floppy-eared BEAR. My toes WIGGLE and JIGGLE HIDDEN under the protective UMBRELLA of my one-piece sunflower YELLA footsie PAJAMAS.

The dark CHERRY wooden RAIL spies with a GLARE as I nervously suck my thumb hiding THERE on those carpeted STAIRS off to the side of the grey slate stone hallway, it shrivels like a prune.

Sodium-drenched HYDROGEN and OXYGEN BEGIN to BLEACH my eyes and warmly caress my CHEEKS. My body impatiently shivers and WEEPS. I cannot SLEEP. So I listen. I WAIT. I am timid and just EIGHT...and quietly invisible in this velvet gold wallpapered semi-dark SPACE. I feel alone.

Muffled voices and the scent of cheap Folger's coffee and dank cigarette smoke SWIFTLY LIFT and curl like a morning dew MIST from the early 70s KITCHEN. I wonder what I'm MISSING. I desperately yearn to be WITH THEM.

So, BUMP BUMP. I shimmy down one step, then two, wanting to be part OF the conversation. BUMP...closer still.

Do I have to try? Feels like I do.

When it comes down to it, I cannot stand to be left out...I still can't...I still can't...do I like me?

267

Dramatic PAUSE.
Ha, perhaps this is the dramatic CAUSE of what ails ME, what
creeps through my thought PROCESSES, what makes me spin,
what makes me feel stuck. Perhaps, it all started on a staircase.

Do I have to try? Feels like I do.

Perhaps this is the source of my FEAR, part of my raccoon-eyes
varnished VENEER, always trying to cover up my INSECURITIES
that I hold NEAR and DEAR. They keep me safe you know, like
those footsie pajamas. And like a child if you tease ME, I sadden
SUDDENLY even though I quickly try to cover up my reaction
and ANXIETY, casually saying it's OKAY. I may even laugh and
PLAY as I hide behind my raccoon SHADES. Perhaps, it all started
on a staircase.

Do I like me?

Perhaps this is a reality TV show "Biggest Scared to not be Liked"
REVEAL? I can almost HEAR the crowd clap and CHEER as the
band plays the theme from "Rocky". Imagine the lights dim LOW
as I hide in the vestiBULE and then make my grand entrance. But
don't expect silky boxer SHORTS with a "Jab Jab CROSS"
exploding from big red GLOVES. And certainly don't expect me to
unveil in black strappy ass heels and a "fuck me" black dress to
show deep cleavage that I'm assuredly PROUD OF. You see, this
isn't your reality show reveal. It all started on a staircase where
that little girl sucked her thumb UNAWARE of the big reveal
going on THERE in that 70s kitchen dusted in coffee grinds and
nicotine. This is just me trying to get to know me a little BETTER.
And if I like me, then I guess that's all that MATTERS.

I wanted them to like me. It all started on a staircase.

Do I like me? YES.

Afterword: Comments about the Redondo Poets Reading

The phone would ring—the landline. It would be francEyE. Was I going to the Coffee Cartel on Tuesday? Because if I was, would I consider giving her a ride? I'd immediately say yes, and tell her I'd pick her up at 6:15. Then I'd hang up and check the calendar and cancel whatever else had been planned. Redondo was far—even from Santa Monica—and traffic was fierce. But the rides with francEyE were precious and she was an excellent navigator for a pedestrian. On the way, we'd talk of life and poetry and on the way back, we'd talk of all that had transpired in the night. It was one of her favorite readings and remains one of mine. I felt incredibly honored to feature there and love that it is just far enough away from LA that it isn't courting glamour, but nurturing great writers. (EA)

I have always cherished my excursions down to Coffee Cartel for the Redondo Poets' Reading Series. I feel so lucky to have featured among such a lively and diverse group of poets and performers. It always feels both incredibly homey and down to earth while a touch exotic for me! (I love any chance to steal away from my home front responsibilities) and always a thrill to participate in the fab show you guys M.C. each month. Never stop is what I'm trying to say. (MB)

I would very much like to thank you for hosting me in your lively and engaging series. I heard some mighty fine words being slung and/or sung (for that matter) on the evenings I have spent with you. (LAB)

Coming up to Redondo with my fellow Orange County Ugly Mug poets is always a blast. I have felt privileged to both feature and just attend. (MC)

It was a great pleasure and honor to read these poems at Coffee Cartel. It's always such a treat to read at Coffee Cartel. (HC)

I cut my teeth at the Redondo Poets reading and would like to give a huge thank you to Jim Doane and Larry Colker, who have tirelessly worked to provide encouragement and a continuous home base to local favorites and itinerant writers for many years. (SC)

I wish I'd known about open mic poetry when I was in High School. The Redondo Poets series has always featured young people speaking their truth to a world that too rarely listens. (TD)

I have enjoyed every reading at Redondo Poets. There is always a great mix of poetry. You never know who is gonna move you and what you will leave feeling. There's always great laughs and a great energy in the crowd of regulars. I particularly love the varying age range of poets this reading draws. Never a dull moment at Redondo Poets. (AD)

I've featured at hundreds of venues in the U.S., Europe, Brazil, and Russia, and nowhere have I found a more comfortable setting or more gracious hosts than the Redondo Poets reading. Long may they run! (JG)

The series has always attracted an incredibly diverse and talented crowd of poets, crossing every age and cultural stratum imaginable. Which makes each Tuesday night reading decidedly alive and vibrant, punctuated with just a dash of espresso-maker background music. (EI)

Poetry Readings Tuesday Eves call Larry for info.
I did. It changed my life.
Off I went, scared as hell. All ages, all backgrounds of poets

270

Sharing their stories and feelings. I was hooked
Two poems 4 minutes that's all you get
In time I brought in my guitar added some jazz and blues to the
   mix
Poetry with the music! What fun!
Got some poems published (to my shock)
Thank you CC.
I am still at it. I hope that some things will never change (RL)

Reading at the Redondo Poets is playing the big time, the Palace, the Apollo—I was so nervous—I upset my coffee all over the floor, my hands shook and the pages rattled—it was wonderful. (JM)

Redondo Poets: No matter how far you have to travel to be there, it's always well worth the trip. (RM)

The Coffee Cartel reading has this odd bell curve. At one node, a cluster of high school and college-aged kids; on the other a squadron of 60-and-over longtime CC habitués—and nothing in between! I would race in from LA for a reading, the toxins seeping out of my pores, look around and go, oh yeah, this is kind of a family place. And yet one must be true to one's crazy id. It was a tricky balance.... One night, riled up about some fling gone awry, I set the landspeed record for the word Fuck. The lightning round ensued and, not missing a beat, the regulars pulled vulgar writs or anecdotes out of their secret spleens, more than taking up the challenge. *Go Redondo Beach, Go!* So much fun here over the years with friends and performers. (KN)

The Redondo Poets reading is unpredictable, anarchistic, embracing, fun. All are welcome and are made to feel so. One can't say that about every corner of the world. Thank you, RP! (CP)

From my first time, in the company of then Redondo native Carine Topal, I have felt throw-the-doors-open welcome to this reading. Larry and Jim do a remarkably graceful and pace-minded job of poet wrangling and bringing a sense of special occasion to each Tuesday night at 8:10. The company is unfailingly eclectic, sometimes brash, a grab bag of delights, appreciative. I never leave without having given away at least one of the poems I read. The sounds and smell of coffee brewing, smoke wafting in from outside, the ambience of artists gathering. In short, I cherish you Coffee Cartel reading. Twenty million thanks, a million per year. (BR)

When I read at the Redondo Beach Poets reading in 2015 I was impressed with the warm and welcoming vibe in the coffee house and among those present to read and listen to poetry. The audience really listened to my work and I felt a mutual enjoyment in the experience. (TS)

I have been featured twice at Coffee Cartel and enjoy the venue and audience and yes, the hosts. I like the diversity of the audience, the young and the older together. (LB)

I'm a longtime student of the Redondo Poets series. I always, ALWAYS, learn something beautiful there. In its twenty-year history, I've watched emerging and established writers find true community and support for their work. (BC)

Two of California's most discerning and hospitable emcees keep the South Bay's spoken word scene firmly anchored in its tradition of fostering newcomers while presenting the best writers/ performers around. There are many of them, and Larry and Jim have given those readers and audiences alike two decades of splendid coffee and community as the sun sets and the mist rolls in from the sea. (AF)

In 2010, I read at Coffee Cartel for Redondo Poets. During the open mic, a poet got up to read his poems but first emphatically stated, "I came here tonight to hear Cece." Better than a Pushcart, I thought. I thank Redondo Poets for making that moment possible. (CP)

Long live the Coffee Cartel which has already lived long. It is truly holy work to foster a weekly creative environment for a wild variety of voices for decades. (RL)

Every poet in Southern California has learned that reading at Coffee Cartel for the Redondo Poets series feels like a family event in its ease and generosity, like the poetry equivalent of a house concert. For me, the only thing better than reading there is listening to my friends when they read there. (DSJ)

On Cecilia Woloch's recommendation I discovered your welcoming and lively and wild reading. My poem "After Midnight" fit in with the mood of the night. My British cousin, Wendy Klein, who also read asked if American readings were always like this. I said "Absolutely not." I fell in love with poetry at El Camino College years before and it was great to meet current Camino students and your diverse group of poets. (PP)

Back on April 6, 2010, Coffee Cartel was my first featured reading ever. I was scared but Larry, Jim and the diverse local crowd were very welcoming and supportive then as well as when I returned. Particularly during these years of shrinking opportunities, Redondo Poets is a major cultural resource for the South Bay. Thank you, thank you! (GS)

Thank you both and congrats on your long running weekly series and your decision to publish an anthology celebrating your achievement!!!! I can only imagine the difficulty of such an endeavor—I have run the monthly Corners of the Mouth since 1984 but it is once a month and I have had Patti helping me these past 17 years. In fact, when we published *Corners of the Mouth: A Celebration of Thirty Years at the Annual San Luis Obispo Poetry Festival*—several years ago we had a blast though it was a hell of a lot of work we did find it exhilarating connecting with poets we had not heard from in years—of course it was also sad that we could not connect with numerous poets we lost all track of—I wish you luck on this endeavor and that you both find all the joy we found on our journey through the past. Thanks again. (KPS)

[I have] attended hundreds, maybe even thousands, of poetry readings. Redondo Poets remains one of my favorites for the their welcoming, all-inclusive atmosphere. They know how to make a poetry reading fun. (GMT)

Congratulations on achieving twenty years of Coffee Cartel continuity. It is certainly an accomplishment that both of you can be proud of, especially since Redondo has always been and continues to be, a warm, vibrant, surprising and fun series! (BY)

The Redondo Poets Coffee Cartel reading is Redondo Beach's cozy home open mic, and let me tell you: if you like poems, nice people, and feeling the warm fuzzies, you want to go here. The energy in this place is like a family dinner table where the elbow jabs are full of love. (NW)

Rachel Abril works from home because she lives in her office cubicle, which is decorated with half-finished art projects and Pottery Barn furniture. She enjoys feeding the two office pack mules, Artemisia and Hyacinthus, causing disarray, and being one with her best friend and fake Facebook spouse Melanie. Her preferred mediums are permanent crayon and Beyoncé gifs. Also all of this is false, except the part about Melanie. That's true.

E. Amato is a published poet, award-winning screenwriter, and established performer currently based in Berlin. She has three poetry collections: *Swimming Through Amber, 5,* and *Will Travel.* Named one of KCET's *LA Letters* "Five Emerging Female Writers," her poetry is included in Tia Chucha Press' *The Coiled Serpent: Poets Arising from the Cultural Quakes & Shifts of Los Angeles,* and *Voices from Leimert Park Redux.* "Four Girls" and "Sketches of Pain" will appear in her new collection, *Daughters of Invention* (Zesty Pubs).

Amy Ball's childhood was full of songs, stories, and imagination. Once a thing of my pre-teen journals, poetry came to revisit me after an unexpected pregnancy and miscarriage kicked me in the emotional pants. Sometimes the hard moments bring the most wonderful things. In this case, words, imagination, connection, laughter (yes, laughter), and healing.

Ellen Bass's poetry includes *Like a Beggar* (Copper Canyon), *The Human Line* (Copper Canyon), and *Mules of Love* (BOA), and she coedited *No More Masks!* (Doubeday), the first major anthology of poetry by women. Her work has been published in The New Yorker, The New York Times Magazine, The American Poetry Review, The New Republic, Ploughshares, and The Kenyon Review. She teaches in the MFA program at Pacific University. Her website is at www.ellenbass.com.

Michelle Bitting's third collection is *The Couple Who Fell to Earth,* named to Kirkus Reviews' Best Books of 2016. She has poems forthcoming or published in The American Poetry Review, Prairie Schooner, Narrative, The New York Times, Vinyl, Plume, diode, the Paris-American, Raleigh Review, AJP, and others. Poems have appeared on Poetry Daily and Verse Daily, have been nominated for Pushcart and Best of the Net prizes, and most recently, The Pablo Neruda American Literary Review and Tupelo Quarterly Poetry contests. Her website is at www.michellebitting.com. "Lupercalia" appeared on *Cultural Weekly.* "Joni Mitchell is not Unconscious!" first appeared on *Linebreak.*

Laurel Ann Bogen is the author of 11 books of poetry and short fiction, the most recent of which, *Psychosis in the Produce Department: New and Selected Poems 1975-2015*, was published by Red Hen Press in 2016. Since 1990, she has been an instructor of poetry and performance for the UCLA Extension Writers' Program, where she received the Outstanding Instructor of the Year. "I Dream the Light of Reason II" and "May 12, 1971" are from *Psychosis in the Produce Department, New and Selected Poems, 1975-2015.*

Lynne Bronstein is a poet, journalist, fiction writer, occasional playwright, and teacher/tutor. Her poetry and fiction have been published in many local and national magazines. She has been nominated for the Pushcart Prize and the Best of the Net Award. She lives in a House of Poets in the San Fernando Valley.

Elena Karina Byrne, author of *Squander* (Omnidawn, 2016), *MASQUE* (Tupelo Press, 2008), and *The Flammable Bird* (Zoo Press, 2002), former 12-year Regional Director of the Poetry Society of America, is a multi-media artist, editor, board member for What Books Press, Poetry Consultant/Moderator for *The Los Angeles Times* Festival of Books, Literary Programs Director for The Ruskin Art Club, and one of the final judges for the Kate/Kingsley Tufts Prizes in poetry. She recently completed a collection of essays entitled, *Voyeur Hour: Meditations on Poetry, Art & Desire.*

Michael Cantin is a poet and sloth fanatic residing somewhere in the wilds of Orange County, California. He writes fitfully between bouts of madness and periods of lucid concern. His poetry has appeared both online and in print. You can find his work in The East Jasmine Review, Melancholy Hyperbole, 50 Haiku, several anthologies, and elsewhere.

Hélène Cardona is the author of seven books, more recently the award-winning bilingual collections *Life in Suspension*, called "a vivid self-portrait as scholar, seer and muse" by John Ashbery, and *Dreaming My Animal Selves*, described by David Mason as "liminal, mystical and other-worldly." Her translations include *Beyond Elsewhere* (Gabriel Arnou-Laujeac), winner of a Hemingway Grant; *Ce que nous portons* (Dorianne Laux); Walt Whitman's *Civil War Writings* for WhitmanWeb, and *Birnam Wood* (José Manuel Cardona). "Woodwork" and "Life in Suspension" are from *Life in Suspension*.

Randy Cauthen, a former carriage tour driver, disc jockey, and first mate of an Erie Canal packet boat, is Professor of English and Poet in Residence at Cal State, Dominguez Hills. His books of poetry are *The Use of Force* and *Slow Night* (Transparent Books, 2014), and he has also published *Black Letters: An Ethnography of Legal Writing*. Originally from Charleston SC, he now lives in Playa del Rey. Both poems here are from *Slow Night*.

Sharyl Collin didn't plan to be a poet but when she became pregnant with an unplanned poem, she decided to keep it. Her poems have appeared in *Switched-On Gutenberg, Waypoints, The Intentional, Wild Goose Poetry, Mason's Road Literary Journal, *82 Review, Mothers Always Write* and *Lummox*. She has completed a full length poetry collection and two chapbook.

Brendan Constantine is the author of four books of poetry. His most recent collection is *Dementia, My Darling* (Red Hen Press, 2016). He has received grants and commissions from the Getty Museum, James Irvine Foundation, and the National Endowment for the Arts. He currently teaches creative writing at the Windward

School in West Los Angeles and regularly offers classes to hospitals, foster homes, veterans, and the elderly.

Kit Courter is a poet, photographer and musician from the coast, mountains and deserts of Southern California. His two chapbooks, *Shasta Cycle* (2002) and *Krado* (2015), were both published by LunarLight Press. Kit has been featured by Cadence Collective online, and is a regular reader at the Redondo Poets open mic at the Coffee Cartel.

Melanie Dalby has the pleasure of working and living in the cubicle next to Rachel's. Her main inspiration for writing comes from a cardboard cutout of Edgar Allan Poe, whose eyes remain in the bathroom of the office. Melanie's favorite activities include organizing pack mule revolutions in Russia, hiding Rachel's permanent crayons, and avoiding all hipsters named Denny. Also all of this is false, except the part about Denny. That's true. https://mammajrchoochoo.wordpress.com/

Amber Douglas is a powerful, magical poet with unique vibrations of comfort. She has had the pleasure & honor of featuring at Redondo Poets several times. Amber has also featured at Two Idiots Peddling Poetry, thanks to Ben & Steve. As well as been the feature in San Luis Obispo at Linnea's Cafe, thanks to KP Sullivan. And also at Cadence Collective, Long Beach, thanks to Sarah Thursday.

John FitzGerald's poems are from *Favorite Bedtime Stories* (Salmon Poetry, 2014).

Amélie Frank's work has appeared in ART/LIFE, Lummox, poeticdiversity.com (earning a 2016 Pushcart Prize nomination), Sparring with Beatnik Ghosts, Levure Littéraire, Edgar Allan Poet, Cultural Weekly, and *Wide Awake: Poets of Los Angeles and Beyond* (Beyond Baroque Books, 2015). Co-founder of the Sacred Beverage Press, she produced the acclaimed literary journal Blue Satellite. Beyond Baroque Literary Arts Center, the Cities of Venice and Los Angeles have honored her for her activism and leadership in the Southern California poetry community.

John Gardiner co-hosted the Laguna Poets workshop, had 12 collections of poems and prose to his credit, taught Shakespeare and creative writing at U.C. Irvine on a part-time basis, and was co-creator of "Shakespeare's Fool," a rock 'n roll presentation of Shakespeare's songs and monologues.

Jessica Goodheart's poetry has appeared in magazines, anthologies and even all together in one book, entitled *Earthquake Season,* published by Word Press (2010). As meaningful to her as any of this is the scrap of paper she retrieved from the hat after her reading at the Coffee Cartel. It reads, "I have no cash. But if I did, I would give it to you. You were wonderful. Michelle." She keeps it with her jewelry. Thank you, Redondo Poets! Thank you, Michelle! Her poems here are from *Earthquake Season.*

Bradford Goodis found writing at the age of sixteen when his father died and he had nowhere to turn but his own thoughts. He grew up in Philadelphia and went on to live in Denver, Miami, San Diego, and Los Angeles, all of which have inspired the novels, poems, and children's books he has written. The Redondo Poets reading at the Coffee Cartel is the first place he ever shared his work, and he tries hard to make it every Tuesday.

Tresha Faye Haefner has lived and worked in Los Angeles for five years. She is grateful to the Coffee Cartel, which has featured her twice, and provided a steady stream of inspiration on Tuesday nights. Tresha is the founder of The Poetry Salon, which provides small, personalized classes and workshops for writers around Los Angeles. Visit her website at www.thepoetrysalon.com to find out more. "The Jungle Tattoo" originally appeared in BloodLotus, Issue #12. "I Will Arise Now and go to Los Angeles" was originally published by Writer's Row and has appeared on Cultural Weekly.

Dina Hardy is the recipient of an MFA from the Iowa Writers' Workshop, a Stegner Fellowship from Stanford University, residencies in Spain and Wales, and a Pushcart Prize nomination. Find her work now or soon in Alaska Quarterly Review, Bennington Review, Pangyrus, Prelude, and Ink Brick—and on her website: dinahardy.com. "Yours Is Everything" first appeared in H-NGM-N.com Issue 18. "[the magician's assistant]" first appeared in *Gulf Coast Journal*, Vol. 28 Issue 2.

Donna Hilbert's books include Transforming Matter, and Traveler in Paradise: New and Selected Poems, both from PEARL Editions. Her work is widely anthologized, including *Boomer Girls, A New Geography of Poets, Solace in So Many Words,* and recently in *The Widows' Handbook* (Kent State University Press) and *The Doll Collection* (Terrapin Books). Poems appear each month in the on-line literary magazine Verse-Virtual.com. More at donnahilbert.com. "Madeleine" and "Domestic Arts" are from *The Green Season* (World Parade Books, 2009).

Jean Barrett Holloway has published *Weightlifting Rules, Poems & Photographs,* and a chapbook, *This World So Frail, Kwajalein Poems* (Conflux Press, 2010). Forthcoming: a new book, *Over the Falls* (Tebot Bach). Additional publications in: Spillway, The Comstock Review, Poetry Bay, Tiger's Eye, the anthology *Beyond the Lyric Moment: Poetry Inspired by Workshops with David St. John,* and the true crime book *Black Dahlia Avenger II.* She is a grateful participant in the poetry workshops of David St. John and Gail Wronsky. "When the Shadows Run South and North" is from *This World So Frail, Kwajalein Poems.*

Eric Howard studied poetry at the Claremont Colleges before moving to Los Angeles to work as a junior high school, high school, and college teacher and later as an editor. He also studied formal verse with Henri Coulette at Cal State LA. Being invited to feature at Coffee Cartel encouraged him to start writing seriously again after a long hiatus. "The Fates on Location" appears in his debut collection, *Taliban Beach Party* (Turtle Point Press, 2017; used with permission).

LeAnne Hunt grew up in the Midwest and lives in Orange County, CA. She is a regular at the Ugly Mug reading in Orange and enjoys the poet exchange between the Ugly Mug and Redondo Poets at Coffee Cartel. She has poems published in

Lummox, Incandescent Mind and Black Napkin Press. She posts prompts at leannehunt.com.

Elizabeth Iannaci is a widely published and anthologized Los Angeles-based poet who remembers when there really were orange groves. She holds an MFA in Poetry, has traveled extensively and read her work in Slovenia, Istanbul, Paris, and New Delhi without getting arrested (knock on wood), and can usually find out how to ask, "Where is the bathroom/water closet/toilet/facilities?" She occasionally writes letters on real paper, delivered by real humans. "All in the Timing" was previously published in Pentimento Magazine. "The Eldest of the Twelve Dancing Princesses Tells..." was first published in Poemeleon. Both had their maiden outing at Coffee Cartel.

Charlotte Innes is the author of *Descanso Drive* (Kelsay Books, 2017), and two chapbooks, *Licking the Serpent* (2011) and *Reading Ruskin in Los Angeles* (2009), both with Finishing Line Press. Her poems have appeared in The Hudson Review, The Raintown Review, and Rattle. She loves the fervor for poetry that makes Coffee Cartel audiences so special. One of her poems once made someone cry! "I Sit Still and Something Happens" first appeared in *Licking the Serpent.* "My Friend the Philosopher" first appeared in Knockout literary magazine in 2010 (winner of Knockout's inaugural poetry contest).

Wendy Klein is the author of *Cuba in the Blood* (2009) and *Anything in Turquoise* (2013), from Cinnamon Press, and *Mood Indigo* (Overstep Books, 2016). She has been published in Envoi, Magma, Smiths Knoll, Brittle Star, the Frogman Papers, Seam, Jewish Renaissance, Oxford Poetry, and Mslexia magazines, along with many anthologies. "Just Jacaranda" is from *Anything in Turquoise.* "The People of Sahel Remember Rain" is from *Mood Indigo.*

Richard Leach is the author of *Quite Noise* and *Vibrato: Poems and Tales,* both from Point Fermin Press. "Salt Air and the Seal" was published in *Aquarium of the Pacific Poetry Contest Winners*

2009 to 2015. "How Many Nights" was published in Overture magazine (American Federation of Musicians Local #47).

Marie C Lecrivain is the executive editor/publisher of poeticdiversity: the litzine of Los Angeles, and a writer-in-residence at her apartment. Her work has appeared in a number of journals, including Edgar Allen Poetry Journal, The Los Angeles Review, Nonbinary Review, Red Fez, Spillway, Orbis, and others. She's the author of several volume of poetry and short stories, including her seventh poetry chapbook, *Fourth Planet From the Sun,* which will be published in 2018 by Rum Razor Press.

Suzanne Lummis has been the principal editor of two landmark anthologies, *Grand Passion: The Poetry of Los Angeles and Beyond* (Red Wind Books, 1995) and *Wide Awake: Poets of Los Angeles and Beyond* (Pacific Coast Poetry Series/Beyond Baroque Books, 2015). A key figure in the Stand-up Poetry movement in the 90s, Lummis is also known for her essays defining the poem noir. She co-founded the Los Angeles Poetry Festival, has written two prize-winning plays, and is an award-winning teacher at UCLA Extension. Her poems have appeared in The New Yorker, Ploughshares, The Hudson Review, New Ohio Review, among others. "When in Doubt Have a Man Come Though the Door with a Gun in His Hand" is from *In Danger* (Roundhouse Press/Heyday Books). "The Night Life Is for You" is from *Open 24 Hours* (Lynx House Press).

Rick Lupert is the 2014 recipient of the Beyond Baroque Distinguished service award. He created the Poetry Super Highway (http://poetrysuperhighway.com) and hosted the weekly Cobalt Cafe reading for almost 21 years. He's authored 21 collections of poetry (most recently *God Wrestler*). He writes the Jewish Poetry Column "From the Lupertverse" for JewishJournal.com and created the daily web comic Cat and Banana with Brendan Constantine. He loves you.

Sarah Maclay's most recent collection is *The "She" Series: A Venice Correspondence*, a braided collaboration with Holaday

Mason (What Books Press, 2016). A 2016 COLA Fellow, 2015 Yaddo resident, and Pushcart Special Mention awardee, her earlier books include *Music for the Black Room (2011), The White Bride* (2008) and *Whore* (2004, Tampa Review Prize for Poetry), all from UT Press. Her poems and criticism appear in APR, The Writer's Chronicle, FIELD, *The Best American Erotic Poetry: From 1800 to the Present,* Ploughshares, Poetry International, where she long served as Book Review Editor, and many other spots. She teaches poetry and creative writing at Loyola Marymount University in Los Angeles. "For You Who Are Not With Me, Who Are With Me" first appeared on poeticdiversity and is collected in *The White Bride.* "At the Thrift Shop Café" appeared in *Beyond the Valley of the Contemporary Poets 2005 Anthology,* later made its Web debut on Poemeleon, and is collected in *Music for the Black Room.*

Ellyn Maybe, Southern California-based poet, United States Artist nominee 2012, has performed nationally and internationally as a solo artist and with her band. Her work has been included in many anthologies and she is the author of numerous books. She also has a critically acclaimed poetry/music album, *Rodeo for the Sheepish* (Hen House Studios). In addition to her band, her latest poetry/music project is called ellyn & robbie. Their new album is called Skywriting with Glitter. Her websites are at ellynmaybe.com and ellynandrobbie.com. "Someday Our Peace Will Come" was originally published for S.A. Griffin's project, *The Poetry Bomb.*

Julianna McCarthy has poems in The Antioch Review, Nimrod, Switched-on Gutenberg, Alehouse, Best Poem. "The Fall" appeared in Icon. "Ars Poetica " appeared in the American Journal of Poetry.

Terry McCarty has written poems in, around—and sometimes about-Los Angeles since 1997. Terry's poems can be found in the anthologies *Beyond the Valley of the Contemporary Poets* (VCP Press 2001 edition), *So Luminous The Wildflowers* (Tebot Bach), *The Long Way Home: The Best of the Little Red Book Series 1998-2008* (Lummox Press) and *Short Poems Ain't Got Nobody To Love*

(For The Love Of Words). "Ode to the Sylmar Bear" appeared on poeticdiversity.

Elaine Mintzer In the 50's poets wore black and spoke their poems in smoky, crowded, dimly-lit clubs to audiences of espresso-drinking beatniks. More than half a century later, Elaine is happy to be among the hipsters at Coffee Cartel, wearing her mom jeans and reading over the noise of cappuccino machines. The smoke is outdoors, courtesy of young vapers. Elaine's book of poetry, Natural Selections, is available through Amazon. "On the Evening News" was published by Mom Egg Review, Volume 15. "Catfish" was published by Cultural Weekly.

Michelle Mitchell-Foust received her Ph.D. in Creative Writing from the University of Missouri-Columbia. She is the author of two poetry books, *Circassian Girl* (Elixir Press) and *Imago Mundi* (Elixir Press), and two chapbooks, *Poets at Seven* (Sutton Hoo Press) and *Exile* (Sangha Press). She has edited two anthologies with Tony Barnstone, *Dead and Undead Poems* and *Monster Verse* (Everyman Press/Knopf, 2014, 2015). "Exponential" appeared in The Colorado Review.

Bill Mohr has a Ph.D. in Literature (University of California, San Diego; 2004) and is a Professor of English at California State University, Long Beach. He has worked as a small press editor and publisher in Los Angeles since 1972 and is also a literary historian and critic. In 2011, the University of Iowa Press published *Holdouts: The Los Angeles Poetry Renaissance 1948-1992*. His first full-length volume of poems, *hidden proofs,* was published in 1982. What Books, an imprint of the Glass Table Collective, will publish *Los Manantiales del Nirvana / The Headwaters of Nirvana* in October, 2018.

Raundi Moore-Kondo is the founder of For The Love of Words Writing Collective, author of two poetry collections, editor/publisher of three all-ages poetry anthologies, singer/songwriter and bassist for the bands, Hurt and The Heartbeat and Daisy Unchained. When she isn't pushing poetry on people or playing music, she can be found photographing phantoms, messing around with mermaids or dancing with dust-devils. Her website is www.theloveofwords.com. "Let's Get Out of Here" and "God Bless Us Everyone" were published in *Death of a Snowman.*

Jim Natal is the author of four poetry collections: *52 Views: The Haibun Variations; Memory and Rain; Talking Back to the Rocks;* and *In the Bee Trees.* A multi-year Pushcart Prize nominee, his poetry has appeared in numerous print and online journals, as well as in many anthologies. He received his MFA from Antioch University–Los Angeles in 2005 after a 25-year career as a creative executive with the National Football League. A longtime workshop leader, literary presenter, and series coordinator, he also runs indie publishing house Conflux Press. "Moses" is from *Talking Back to the Rocks* (Archer Books, 2003). "Rock, Earth, Wood" is from *In the Bee Trees* (Archer Books, 2000).

Keith Niles' poesy can be found online at sites like Underground Voices and Poetic Diversity, offline in places such as Artillery Magazine, Caffeine, plus sundry small zines, and on video via youtube.com. He was the host of the open mic at the Little Joy in the late aughts. His current band and longtime poetry imprint share the same aesthetic: *Know nothing.*

Kim Noriega's poems have appeared in textbooks, journals, and anthologies including *American Life in Poetry, Verse Daily,* and *The Tishman Review.* She was a semi-finalist in 2016 for the James Baker-Hall Memorial Prize in Poetry and a finalist for the 2017 Edna St. Vincent Millay Poetry Prize. Kim's poetry collection, *Name Me,* was published by Fortunate Daughter Press in 2010. She lives in San Diego where she heads the library's award-winning family literacy program. It's nothing but a vicious rumor that she keeps all her books in Dewey Decimal number order at home, but those other things you've heard, well, they're probably true. "Name Me" was originally published in Paris Atlantic.

Judith Pacht's *Summer Hunger* won the 2011 PEN Southwest Book Award for Poetry. A three-time Pushcart nominee, she was first place winner in the Georgia Poetry Society's Edgar Bowers competition. Pacht's work has been published in journals that include Ploughshares, Runes, Nimrod and Phoebe, and her poems were translated into Russian where they appeared in Foreign Literature (Moscow, Russia). Her work appears in numerous anthologies. Pacht has read at the Los Angeles Times Festival of Books, at Charleston's Piccolo Spoleto Festival, and has read and taught Political Poetry at Denver's annual LitFest at the Lighthouse. "Spider" appears in *Just a Little More Time* (DCV Press, 2017), an anthology on love and loss.

Candace Pearson grew up in the "other" California—the great Central Valley. She now scratches out her poems in a 1900s hiking cottage in the foothills of Altadena. A multiple Pushcart Prize nominee, she has had work published in leading journals and anthologies. Her collection, *Hour of Unfolding* (Briery Creek Press, 2010), won the Liam Rector First Book Prize for Poetry from Longwood University. "Coffee Break" was first published in *Hour of Unfolding.*

Cece Peri's poems have appeared in Malpais Review, Luvina: The LA Issue, Askew, and in the anthologies *Beyond the Lyric Moment* (Tebot Bach, 2014), *Master Class: The Poetry Mystique* (Duende Books, 2015), and *Wide Awake: Poets of Los Angeles and Beyond* (Beyond Baroque Books, 2015). She received the first Anne Silver Poetry Award and awards from NoirCon 2012 and Arroyo Arts Collective's 2014 "Poetry in the Windows." Originally from New York, she has lived in the Los Angeles area since 2003. Trouble Down the Road" was first published in Malpais Review (Winter 2012-2013). "The White Chicken Gives a First Hand Account" was first published by Writers at Work as Poem of the Month, September 2009.

Penny Perry's "501 Valley Drive" was first published in the *San Diego Poetry Annual.* "After Midnight" was first published in her poetry collection *Santa Monica Disposal and Salvage.*

Bren Petrakos has had words in her mind. Words which tend to escape, running past borders, jumping fences, causing loud fuss and uncomfortable silences. She makes no apology. But is grateful for the tolerance and open minds, hearts, and overall wonder of the Coffee Cartel.

Darby Power is currently pursuing her undergraduate degree in Creative Writing from Vanderbilt University. She loves words, her dog Louie, and adventures with no destination. She has frequented Coffee Cartel's Poetry Night since she was in high school, and firmly believes that a Tuesday night spent anywhere else is incomplete. Without Redondo Poets, most of her poems would not exist. "love letter to everything I am and someday will be" was first published in *Rules*.

Marilyn N. Robertson has poems in Boston Literary Magazine; *Chopin with Cherries, A Tribute in Verse*; ASKEW; Poem of the Month for Writers at Work; the anthology *Wide Awake: Poets of Los Angeles and Beyond;* and online at Speechlessthemagazine.org and Capitalandmain.com. Selected for *Poetry in the Windows*, a grant project of the Arroyo Arts Collective, one of her poems was displayed on a poster in the window of a business on Figueroa St. in Northeast LA. UCLA Extension featured her in a success-stories series.

Beth Ruscio is a poet, daughter of actors, accomplished actress (*Dreamland, 28 Days, View From The Bridge*), mentor (Otis School of Art and Design), finalist (Two Sylvia Prize, Sunken Garden Poetry Prize, The Wilder Prize, Tupelo Quarterly Prize, Ruth Stone Poetry Prize), published (California Journal of Poetics, Cultural Weekly, Tupelo Quarterly, Spillway, Speechlessthemagazine.org, In Posse, Malpais Review), anthologized (*Beyond The Lyric Moment, Conducting A Life: Maria Irene Fornes, Poet's Calendar*), and persistent. "Imaginary Memorial" and "Non Grata" were published in California Journal of Poetics, Issue 2.

Cathie Sandstrom is a military brat who still expects to hear from the Pentagon any day. She has lived in ten states and four foreign countries. Her work has appeared in *The Southern Review, Ploughshares, Lyric, Comstock Review, Ekphrasis,* and is published by the Academy of American Poets on poets.org. Anthologies include *Wide Awake: Poets of Los Angeles and Beyond.* Her poem "You, Again" is in the J. Paul Getty Museum artists' book collection.

Gerard Sarnat was nominated for a 2016 Pushcart Prize. He's authored *HOMELESS CHRONICLES, Disputes, 17s,* and *Melting The Ice King* (2016), which included work published in Gargoyle and Lowestoft. Mount Analogue selected Sarnat's "KADDISH FOR THE COUNTRY" for distribution as a pamphlet on Inauguration Day 2017, and as part of the Washington/nationwide Women's Marches. Gerry has built and staffed clinics for the marginalized, been a CEO of healthcare organizations, and been a Stanford professor of Medicine. His website is at GerardSarnat.com.

Diana Sieker was born and raised in Redondo Beach. She was first a Seahawk at Redondo Union High School, then an Anteater at the University of California, Irvine, and now she is a Mustang at Mira Costa High School, where she has taught English for the past 12 years. Her students first brought her to Coffee Cartel in 2010, and nothing makes her happier than watching her students perform and kill it on the microphone.

Linda Singer had a small role in Roy Rogers' last movie, has had two plays produced in Dallas, sold a script to the TV series Evening Shade and currently performs with the Acting Troupe, Stop Senior Scams. She has featured at several Southern California poetry venues, has been published in a variety of journals and had a joke published in Reader's Digest. She thinks of Redondo Poets as a breeding ground for young talent.

Graham Smith, of Long Beach, is known to be partial to three-line poems and pints of Guinness.

Joan Jobe Smith, CSULB and UCI MFA grad, founding editor of Pearl litmag and Bukowski Review, has published internationally in more than 1000 journals, newspapers, anthologies, her first poem at age 10 winner of a Red Cross poster contest appearing on billboards across USA. Her prose memoir *Tales of an Ancient Go-Go Girl* was published in 2014, and in 2017 New York Quarterly will publish *Moonglow à Go-Go: New & Selected Poetry.*

Wanda VanHoy Smith joined the Redondo Poets workshop early on, and was a regular at the readings into her late 80s. She penned three books for young people, two collections of poetry, and a multitude of chapbooks. She is remembered for her witty poems about Los Angeles icons and jazz, and for her verve. "Carnal Knowledge of a Tomato" is from her chapbook, *It's About Time.* "Teddy Bears Don't Talk" appeared in *51%.*

David St. John's most recent collection is *The Last Troubadour: New and Selected Poems* (Ecco, 2017). "The Opal Trees" and "Bumble Bee" were first published in the collection *PRISM* (Arctos Press, 2002).

Terry Stevenson is a recovering attorney having retired after serving for 37 years in the Burbank City Attorney's Office. I have had the good fortune of studying with some fine poets, among them Jack Grapes, David St. John, Suzanne Lummis, and Gail Wronsky. My poems have appeared in Electrum, Poetry/LA., Rattle, Spillway and ONTHEBUS. I have been published in the anthologies *Shards, Off-Ramp, Corners* (all published by the Pasadena Poets), *The New Los Angeles Poets* (Bombshelter Press), *Truth and Lies that Press for Life* (Artifact Press, Ltd.), *13 LA Poets* (Bombshelter Press), *So Luminous the Wildflowers: An Anthology of California Poets* (Tebot Bach), *Good Poems: American Places* (Garrison Keillor, Ed., Viking), *Beyond the Lyric Moment: Poetry Inspired by Workshops with David St. John, Master Class: The Poetry Mystique* (Suzanne Lummis, Ed., Duende Books), and *Went to Ralph's to Get A Chicken* (poems for Jack Grapes) (BAMBAZ Press).

Kevin Patrick Sullivan's books include *First Sight, The Space Between Things*, and *Under Such Brilliance*. His poems are in SOLO, ASKEW, MIRAMAR, several anthologies, and online at Other Voices International. He is the co-editor of the anthology *Corners of the Mouth: A Celebration of Thirty Years at the Annual San Luis Obispo Poetry Festival*. He is co-founder, director and curator of the Annual San Luis Obispo Poetry Festival. "Blue Sky" was first published in *First Sight* (Mille Grazie Press). "Sleepers" was first published in Hummingbird.

Paul Suntup's poetry has appeared in numerous publications including Forklift, Ohio; Rattle; ART/LIFE; Cider Press Review; ISM; and the anthology *180 More: Extraordinary Poems for Every Day*, edited by Billy Collins. His first full-length book of poetry, *Sunset at the Temple of Olives*, was published in 2011 by Write Bloody Publishing. He was born in South Africa and currently resides in Southern California. "The Painter" and "Haystack" appeared in Forklift, Ohio Issue #34 (Fall 2016).

G. Murray Thomas founded and published *Next...*, the monthly 'zine of the Southern California poetry scene (later incorporated into Poetix.net). "Charlie Brown in the Strip Club" originally appeared on poeticdiversity.com. "Your Kidney Just Arrived at LAX" originally appeared in Chiron Review.

Lynne Thompson is the author of *Start With A Small Guitar* and *Beg No Pardon*, winner of the Perugia Press Book Award. Winner of the 2016 Stephen Dunn Poetry Prize for her poem "Politics," Thompson's work has recently appeared or is forthcoming in the African American Review, Prairie Schooner, Poetry, and Crab Creek Review. "Siren" first appeared in Ecotone (Fall 2015). "Binding" first appeared in Fourteen Hills (2015).

Carine Topal is a transplanted New York City poet. She refuses, however, to give up her accent, regardless of the years she's been in California. She's taught hither and yon, and has settled down— in her final 30 poetic years—in the Southern California desert. She teaches writing workshops and performs her work in the Palm

Springs and Redondo Beach areas. "Of Man, Woman, Snake, Fruit," was originally published by Mid-America Review (2008). "The Favourite Poet, 1888," won the Robert G. Cohn Prose Poetry Award in 2008, and was included in a special-edition chapbook entitled *Bed of Want,* published by Black Zinnias (an imprint of California Institute of Arts and Letters). Carine's fourth collection, *Tattooed,* won the 2015 Palettes & Quills 4th Biennial Chapbook Contest. Her new poetry collection, *In Order of Disappearance,* was selected for the poetry manuscript award by the Pacific Coast Poetry Series, an imprint of Beyond Baroque Books, and was published in January, 2018.

Kathleen Tyler taught for many years, and now works occasionally as a stable hand and essay scorer. Her publications include *Open the Window and Drown* from Kelsay Books, *My Florida* from Backwaters Press, and *The Secret Box* from Mayapple Press. Her poems have appeared in numerous journals including Quiddity, Women Write Resistance Anthology, The Rattling Wall (Pen/USA), Visions International, Runes, Solo, Poetry Motel, Margie, Seems, Cider Press Review, and others. *Open the Window and Drown* was a finalist for the Brighthorse Prize in Poetry. Her website is at kathleentyler.com.

Rolland Vasin, CPA (*aka* Vachine), reads at open mics nationwide, featuring at leading Los Angeles literary venues. Published in anthologies and journals, he was honored as an Aloud Series Emerging Los Angeles Poet and recognized at the Laugh Factory as the third funniest CPA in LA. When not writing, or auditing children's charities, he resides in Santa Monica, where he plays guitars and banjos but not at the same time.

Fred Voss, a machinist in Southern California machine shops for 38 years, has had three collections of poetry published by Bloodaxe Books, the latest of which, *Hammers and Hearts of the Gods,* was selected a Book of the Year 2009 by The Morning Star. In 2016 he won the Port of Los Angeles-Long Beach Labor Coalition's Joe Hill Labor Poetry Award, and his latest book,

The Earth and the Stars in the Palm of Our Hand, is published by Culture Matters, with a foreword by Len McCluskey, General Secretary of Unite the Union.

Pam Ward's first novel, *Want Some Get Some,* (Kensington) chronicles LA after the '92 riots. Her second novel, *Bad Girls Burn Slow* (Kensington) is about a female serial killer working the funeral circuit. A UCLA graduate and recipient of a California Arts Council Fellow, A New Letters Literary Award and a Pushcart nominee for poetry, Pam published the first anthology on Los Angeles Black women poets, *The Supergirls Handbook.* She operates a graphic design studio and runs her own community press called Short Dress Press. Pam produced the interactive show, "My Life, LA" documenting black Angelenos in poster stories. Her poetry performance "I Didn't Survive Slavery for This!" was featured in the the Leimert Park Theater Festival. Pam just completed her fourth novel, *I'll Get You, My Pretty,* based on the true story of her aunt Mattie, a black actress who dated the prime Black Dahlia suspect. Her website is at www.pamwardwriter.com. "Sunflower Seeds" was published in the Los Angeles Times (2013).

Charles Harper Webb's latest book of poems is *Brain Camp* (University of Pittsburgh Press, 2015). *A Million MFAs Are Not Enough,* a collection of Webb's essays on contemporary American poetry, was published by Red Hen Press (2016). Recipient of grants from the Whiting and Guggenheim foundations, Webb teaches Creative Writing at California State University, Long Beach. "Bouba and Kiki" was first published in River Styx. "Princess Summer-Fall-Winter-Spring" was first published in New Ohio Review.

Hilda Weiss is the co-founder and curator for www.Poetry.LA, a website featuring videos of poets and poetry venues in Southern California. (Redondo Poets at Coffee Cartel is the venue where Poetry.LA began its videotaping project in 2007.) Hilda's chapbook, *Optimism About Trees,* was nominated for a Pushcart prize in 2011. Her poetry has been published in journals such as Askew, Poemeleon, Rattle, and Salamander, and in several anthologies. "Horse's Skull with Pink Rose" was first published in Ekphrasis.

Cecilia Woloch is the author of six collections of poems, most recently *Carpathia* (BOA Editions, 2009) and *Earth* (Two Sylvias Press, 2015), as well as a novel, *Sur la route* (Quale Press, 2015). Her awards include, among others, a fellowship from the National Endowment for the Arts, a Pushcart Prize, and prizes from Indiana Review and New Ohio Review. Based in Los Angeles, she spends half of each year on the road and leads workshops for writers throughout the U.S. and around the world. "Lucifer, Full of Light" is from *Narcissus,* selected by Marie Howe as winner of the 2006 Snowbound Series Chapbook Award (Tupelo Press, 2008). "My Face" is from *Earth,* winner of the 2014 Two Sylvias Press Chapbook Prize.

Sholeh Wolpé was born in Iran. A recipient of the 2014 PEN/Heim, 2013 Midwest Book Award, 2010 Lois Roth Persian Translation prize, her publications include four collections of poetry, two plays, three books of translations, and three anthologies. Wolpé 's modern translation of *The Conference of the Birds* (W.W. Norton) by the 12th century Iranian mystic poet, Attar, has been hailed by Reza Aslan as "timeless as the masterpiece itself." "The Chill" and "The Prince" are from *Keeping Time with Blue Hyacinths* (University of Arkansas Press).

Nancy Lynée Woo is an incorrigible optimist, a 2015 PEN Center USA Emerging Voices Fellow, and a co-founder of the Long Beach Literary Arts Center. She's been ecstatic to be invited for a visit to the Redondo Poets at Coffee Cartel each time she's published a chapbook (which is twice). "The Rescue" was first published on penwheel.lit and then in *Rampant* (Sadie Girl Press, 2014).

Tim Xonnelly RUHS '81, Hermosa Friends of the Arts, Angel's Gate, Beyond Baroque Workshop, Shattersheet & The Moment, La Val's Subterranean, Berkeley Poetry Festival, Coffee Mill, Pegasus

Bookstore, Oakland Review, Cross Strokes: Poetry Between
SF & LA, zines & chapbooks lost. "Carl wants to take me up on it
seven years later and cockeyed drunk" was originally published in
Fustercluck. "These Are My Dumb Socks" was originally
published in Poems on the Emery-Go-Round.

Brenda Yates is the author of *Bodily Knowledge* (Tebot Bach
2015). Her publication credits include Mississippi Review, The
American Journal of Poetry, Tor House News, *City of the Big
Shoulders: An Anthology of Chicago Poetry* (University of Iowa
Press), and *The Southern Poetry Anthology, Volume VI: Tennessee*
(Texas Review Press). Among her awards are the Beyond Baroque
Literary Arts Center Poetry Prize and the Patricia Bibby Memorial
Prize. "Possibilities" appeared in Blueline (Volume XXXVII, Spring
2016). "Animal-flower ABC's" appeared in DASH Literary Journal
(Volume 8, Spring 2015).

James Ysidro has been attending the Redondo Poets reading since
the early 13th Century, back when it was mostly jousting and bear
baiting. He lives very far away; and it takes many hours of hard
riding upon his trusty steed across treacherous bandit-besieged
trails for him to reach it. *'Well worth it!!!'* he will tell you—should
you ever ask.

Mariano Zaro is the author of four books of poetry: *Where
From/Desde Donde, Poems of Erosion/Poemas de la erosión, The
House of Mae Rim/La casa de Mae Rim,* and *Tres letras/Three
Letters.* His poems are included in the anthologies *Monster Verse*
(Penguin Random House), *Wide Awake: Poets of Los Angeles and
Beyond* (Beyond Baroque), *The Coiled Serpent* (Tía Chucha Press),
Angle of Reflection (Arctos Press), and in several magazines in
Spain, Mexico, and the United States. "The Actor" appeared
in LARB (Los Angeles Review of Books, Fall 2016). "Taxi Driver"
appeared in Askew (Summer 2011).

Felice Zoota-Lucero considers herself a poet in disguise. Are her
pieces poems or stories? She will never tell. A Business Analyst
and Software Designer by day, writing and performing are her

creative outlets. She has been a feature poet with Redondo Poets in Redondo Beach, CA, and Poetry Bleeding in Long Beach, CA. Her poems have been published in In-Flight Literary Magazine, Issue 10, found at inflightlitmag.com, and in the anthology *Intersection.*

Made in the USA
San Bernardino, CA
29 March 2018